BRUSSELS
THROUGH COMIC STRIPS

COMIC STRIPS THROUGH
BRUSSELS

A JOURNEY OF DISCOVERY

© 2004 Versant Sud
Rampe du Val, 34
B-1348 Louvain-la-Neuve
Tel. : 32.10.45.51.44
Fax : 32.10.45.51.94
info@versant-sud.com
www.versant-sud.com

Graphic design and page make-up:
Martine d'Andrimont - ARTifice
artifice@skynet.be, Louvain-la-Neuve

Translated from the French by
Rosamund Wilson

Printed in Belgium

D/2004/9445/25
ISBN 2-9303-58-24-6

BRUSSELS
THROUGH COMIC STRIPS
COMIC STRIPS THROUGH
BRUSSELS

A JOURNEY OF DISCOVERY

Thibaut VANDORSELAER

Introduction by Jean VAN HAMME

Versant Sud

If I say Venice, Manhattan, Zanzibar, Acapulco or Samarkand, you start dreaming. Exoticism, adventure, being away from home, mystery or romance. If I mentioned Brussels...

For those who have never stayed there, Brussels is not particularly evocative. Mannekin-Pis, the European Union headquarters, the Grand-Place, perhaps the Atomium, the destructive town-planning between the 1950s and1970s, even the Anderlecht football team... It is hardly inspiring, but in fact, that impression is unfortunate and inaccurate. Brussels is the greenest capital city in Europe and flaunts its charms. The city brims with cultural activities, and the parks that inspire meandering walks are only a tram ride away. So too, is the welcome of the locals, with a *zwanze*, a smile, always on their lips... An old Brussels man said 'Brussels is a city that's stuffed full of secret pleasures'.

For many Europeans, however, Brussels is first and foremost the capital of Belgium. Our small country is always declared to be the spiritual home, not only of Belgian beer and lace, but also of comic strip art. Numerous comic strip artists, whether Belgian or international, French or Flemish-speaking, were right when they gave in to the temptation to locate in Brussels one or more sequences of the stories that they bring to life. The present work by Thibaut Vandorselaer takes pleasure in opening your eyes to the many truly thrilling examples of this art.

However, that is not all. Fifteen or so years ago, the Brussels authorities, in collaboration with the newly-formed Belgian Comic Strip Centre, made a decision to create a living showcase of our 'paper cinema' in the streets. This was because people recognised the special place that Brussels holds in the history of the comic strip, the '9th art form'. Initially a source of inspiration, Brussels was to become its support, literally. So, in the past fifteen years, almost thirty gable-end walls, once blank spaces, were transformed into extraordinary murals dedicated to the heroes in comic strips.

Full of enthusiasm and combining the two main elements of his research, the city and its comic art, Thibaut Vandorselaer has consciously committed himself to mapping out a walk that will take you round the whole city centre with his book in your hand. This walking tour may lead you to the real places that are illustrated by our artists, or to discover their talents on the giant screens of the buildings. If you are a comic strip lover, you will be enchanted; and if you don't enjoy stories that are told 'in little bubbles', go round the city anyway! You will discover a totally different heart to Brussels from the one that traditional guidebooks offer.

Enjoy your walk!

Jean Van Hamme

© Geluck

ITINERARY

This walking tour forms a circular route with 60 stages. Consequently, it is possible to start at any of the stopping-off points. The tour will take between a few hours and a full day depending on whether you make a few, or several stops en route. As a starting point, we suggest the Cathédrale des Saints-Michel-et-Gudule on the Boulevard de l'Impératrice

© De Rouck Cartographie

COMING FROM THE GARE CENTRALE (CENTRAL STATION) YOU WILL SEE THE CATHÉDRALE DES SAINTS-MICHEL-ET-GUDULE TO YOUR RIGHT. THIS IS OUR STARTING POINT

1

The Cathedral is particularly impressive (110m in length, 50m wide and 69m high) because it incorporates three architectural styles: Romanesque, Gothic and Renaissance. Its construction took more than three hundred years (13th – 16th Centuries) to complete.

Barelli's Adventures: Bubbly Brussels, DE MOOR Bob

Bubbly Brussels, one of Barelli's adventures, was written in 1990 at the request of the Ministry of Public Health and Brussels affairs of the Flemish Community. Barelli, the hero, is a young actor. After a long trip abroad he shows young people round Brussels when he makes a visit to stay with his aunt in the capital. Through this comic strip, the city is shown off to advantage thanks to the illustrations of various Flemish institutions' buildings, amongst others. The illustra-

tion above reflects this intention: note the importance that is given to the Flemish Community Administration building in comparison with the Cathedral. Bob de Moor tried to respect the location and the surroundings. The only difference from 'our' reality comes from the fact that the Cathedral's façade has been recently renovated (completed in 1999), restoring it to its former glory.

BOB DE MOOR
[1925-1992]

Bob de Moor, the comic scriptwriter and artist, started his working life in an animated design studio (AFIM). Subsequently he worked for *Kuifje*, the Flemish equivalent of the *Tintin* comic. From 1950 onwards, he became Hergé's first assistant at the Hergé Studios. This work inspired him to create his hero, Barelli. His stories were published by Éditions du Lombard, where he became artistic director in 1989. He also presided over the Administrative Committee of the CBBD (the Belgian Comic Strip Centre) until his death in 1992.

2

Here you will find the Gaston de Franquin character to show you the way. This statue was installed in 1996 to commemorate 100 years of comic strips.

BD Meurtres (Comic Strip Murders) is one of the most recent comic books featuring Ric Hochet. He is involved in a sensitive enquiry: a series of attacks, cases of arson and crimes that are disrupting the world of comic strips. Having narrowly avoided an attack himself, he exposes the criminal. Tibet represents the locations that he uses as the settings for his stories in an accurate way.

TIBET
[1931]

Tibet, the storyline writer and artist, started out as an assistant animator in the Walt Disney studio in Brussels. In 1951, he worked as a mock-up artist on the *Tintin* magazine and created his first complete story, based on one of Duchâteau's storylines. In 1953, he completed the first Chick Bill adventures. Two years later, again with Duchâteau, he started work on the Rick Hochet series. Currently, Tibet continues to keep his two heroes, Chick Bill and Rick Hochet, at the centre of new adventures.

ANDRÉ-PAUL DUCHÂTEAU
[1925]

André-Paul Duchâteau, the comic storyline writer and novelist, published his first novel at the age of fifteen. This was followed by a numerous stories. His first comic strip scripts were published in 1948 in the *Bravo* and *Mickey et Tintin* comics, of which he subsequently became the editor-in-chief. In 1951, he started working with comic strip artists such as Christian Denayer, Daniel Hulet and William Vance. Duchâteau can be considered to be one of the greatest French-speaking Belgian scriptwriters for comics: he has several hundred stories to his credit.

Ric Hochet : B.D. Meurtres, TIBET - A.P. DUCHÂTEAU

At number 20, on your right, you will see the Belgian Comic Strip Centre (CBBD). Since 1989, the CBBD has occupied the Wauques family's former fabric department store. The building that housed the business was designed by Victor Horta in 1903. Nowadays the building is considered to be one of the main cultural and tourist highlights in Belgium. Since 1996, the centenary of the creation of Belgian comic strips, the Centre has had 250,000 visitors a year. The CBBD has non-profit making status and has two main aims: to promote the art of comic strips and to safeguard the centrepiece of Art Nouveau architecture which houses the Centre. Equally, it fulfils a function of providing information and entertainment, by providing visitors with a unique impression of comic strips (BDs) and of Brussels itself. At the Centre there are permanent exhibitions – 'The Development of a Comic Strip', 'The Museum of Make-believe', 'The Museum of Modern Comic Strips' and 'The Victor Horta Gallery', in addition to semi-permanent exhibitions. The Centre also organises and promotes creativity. It presents the Prix du Lion (The Lion Prize) to one or several new comic storyline writers and artists. The financial support for the Centre for Comic Strips comes from different sources: 5% of its

De avonturen van Nero : Het spook uit de zandstraat, Marc SLEEN

funds come from state grants, with the remainder coming from visitor entry charges, the rental of galleries, commercial premises, and various commercial sponsorships.

De avonturen van Nero : Het spook uit de zandstraat, Marc SLEEN

In the storyline that is presented above, it is just before midnight and Nero is leaving a reception in honour of a retrospective exhibition at the CBBD. While he is admiring the Horta building, he hears shouts from the other side of the road from inside the old Presses Socialistes (Socialist Press) building, so he decides to hide behind the wall. He meets an unhappy ghost and he agrees to take its place for a while. During the night, two thieves come to hide their loot after a hold-up and Nero races off to the police with it. This action involves him in a whole host of adventures.

IF YOU GO INTO THE COMIC STRIP CENTRE BUILDING, YOU CAN ENJOY THE ART NOUVEAU INTERIOR AND DISCOVER THE MANY FACETS OF THE ART OF COMIC STRIP-MAKING. BELOW, THERE ARE SEVERAL ILLUSTRATIONS WHICH DEPICT THE INTERIOR OF THE CBBD.

4

De avonturen van Nero : De verloren zee, Marc SLEEN

MARC SLEEN
[1922]

Marc Sleen, the comic scriptwriter and artist, started out as a caricaturist with various Flemish newspapers. In 1947, he created a detective series whose main hero was the detective, Van Zwam. His assistant, Nero, steals the show from him in the fourth episode. From that point onwards, Nero becomes the hero of his own adventures. Marc Sleen produces clear, amusing and imaginative drawings. Between 1951 and 1987, the series was published in French (Néron), initially by Éditions de la Cité, and subsequently by Éditions Érasme.

De avonturen van Nero : De verloren zee, Marc SLEEN

Ric Hochet : B.D. Meurtres, TIBET - A.P. DUCHÂTEAU

Several illustrations show the interior of the Comic Strip Centre.

In *BD Meurtres (Comic Strip Murders)*, Ric Hochet is invited to a reception at the CBBD. While he is there, he witnesses the theft of an incomplete comic strip. This strip had been started by an artist who has just died under mysterious circumstances. Ric Hochet tries to catch the thief because this stolen strip may further his investigation. The illustration gives an accurate representation of the foyer of the Comic Strip Centre. (Note Tintin's rocket and statue on each side of the staircase).

In *De Verloren Zee (The Lost Sea)*, Nero's son invents a submarine and invites his father to go with him into the deepest oceans, in order to beat the world diving record. They encounter extraordinary fish, but they also notice serious pollution in the deep water. At about 10,000 metres Nero starts to experience hallucinations. This is how he discovers the CBBD, where Neptune and his mermaids hold court. The Centre is easily recognisable from the lamp standard and the expansive glass-work. The illustration, while being far from identical to the real building, is clearly based on it.

L'ART NOUVEAU

Art Nouveau architecture was developed at the end of the 19th Century, during the same period as the industrialisation of Belgium. This design style found its beginnings in the work of the architects Victor Horta, Paul Hankar and Henry van de Velde. The Art Nouveau style is characterised by the opening-up of space, the appearance of large bay windows, glass ceilings, the visible use of ironwork, stone and wood, as well as curving architectural lines. The Belgian Comic Strip Centre is a magnificent example of Art Nouveau.

Victor Horta also designed the Palais des Beaux-Arts (see stage 58) and the Gare Centrale (see stage 60) which was inspired by the Art Deco movement.

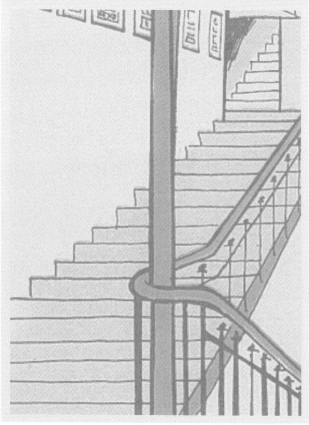

WHEN YOU LEAVE THE CBBD, TURN RIGHT ALONG THE RUE DES SABLES. AT THE T JUNCTION, TURN LEFT INTO THE RUE DU MARAIS AND SHARP RIGHT INTO THE RUE DU PERSIL, BRINGING YOU TO THE PLACE DES MARTYRS. WITH THE SQUARE TO THE RIGHT, GO INTO THE RUE DES ŒILLETS, AND STOP AT THE RUE DES CHOUX (THE FIRST CROSSROADS).

5

Opposite you, at 23, Rue de Damier, you will find the 'Sleep Well' hostel. The reception area is decorated with two murals by Johan de Moor, Bob de Moor's son. As the murals are inside the hotel, they do not represent a stopping-off point as such. However, there is nothing to prevent you from going inside to look at them if you wish.

These two murals represent a double theme: Brussels and comic strip art. In terms of the city, there are interpretations of the landmarks such as the Atomium, the Théâtre de la Monnaie and the Palais de Justice (Law Courts). Also, there are elements of Brussels' culture like the number 33 tram, referring to one of Jacques Brel's songs, a puppet from the Toon theatre (see stage 18), as well as references to Belgian specialities like 'frites' and 'stoemp'. As far as the comic strips are concerned, you can see the Tintin and Snowy characters from Éditions du Lombard (see stage 18), the Marsupilami, the Cow, Tintin's rocket, the Cat, the yellow M sign...

JOHAN DE MOOR
[1953]

Johan de Moor, Bob de Moor's son and Willy Vandersteen's godson, was passionate about drawing from a very young age. In 1981, he joined the Hergé Studios where, in 1983, he took over the artistic direction of 260 short animated cartoons with *Quick and Flupke*, the Brussels 'ketjes' ('youngsters'). After his father's death in 1992, Johan completed the last strips for Bob's final book, *Dali Capitan* (Cori le Moussaillon). Currently, Johan is working on a free adaptation in comic strip form of *The Jungle Book* by Rudyard Kipling.

Turn left along the Rue aux Choux (or if you are coming from the Sleep Well hostel, turn left as you come out of the building, then take the first road on the right). You will find yourself on the Rue Neuve, opposite the Finistère Church. Next, take the Rue du Pont-Neuf to the right of the Church. Keep walking until you reach the Rue de Laeken (the sixth road on the right).

6

On the corner of the Rue du Pont-Neuf and the Rue de Laeken (on your right), you will find the *Spike and Suzy (Bob et Bobette, Suske en Wiske)* mural by Willy Vandersteen.

This work represents a human pyramid that is made up of the main characters in the *Spike and Suzy* adventures. From top to bottom you can see: Suzy and Muffin, Spike, Sidonia, Ambrose and Jethro. At the base, Manneken-Pis, like Jethro, is supporting the human pyramid with one arm. This emblem features on the back of all the comic books.

WILLY VANDERSTEEN
[1913-1990]

Willy Vandersteen, the artist and comic strip writer, was inspired by Hergé and Bob de Moor. His style was clear and easy to read. The adventures of *Spike and Suzy* appeared for the first time in 1945 in de Nieuwe Standaard newspaper, entitled Rikki en Wiske, later becoming *Suske en Wiske* (the Flemish version of *Spike and Suzy*).

THE MURALS

The non-profitmaking *Mural Art Company* has produced all the murals in Brussels using the artists' original work.

Techniques : these depend on the wall that is chosen (its state, scale...) and on the type of work that is to be reproduced. However, it is possible to make generalisations about the usual process which generally has five following stages:

1. Sanding, removing the flaking areas of the supporting base and treatment of possible hinges etc.)

2. Rendering and plastering

3. Fixing of the base and canvas

4. Techniques for increasing the size of the works:

- each artist produces a project to scale

- the work is scanned and the outline is increased to the desired dimensions

- transfers are made on stencils (90 x 350 cm.)

- alignment and piercing of the stencils

- positioning and assembly of the work on the wall followed by the application of the drawing

5. The completion of the work using acrylic paint for exterior use

Choice of walls and designers: Mural Art only works on a consultancy basis. The walls are chosen by Brussels City Council by means of six main criteria:

- gable walls that are neither available for rebuilding nor demolition

- location within Brussels

- the location of other decorated walls

- the use of Art Mural's expertise and technical reports

- the feasibility of the project

- available finance

The artists are chosen co-operatively by Brussels City and the CBBD. Several criteria for the choice of designers come into the equation (among others): they must be

- Belgian, with a special interest in Brussels

- well-known, nationally or internationally

- historically or currently prominent in terms of the art of comic strips

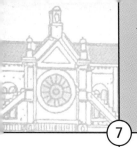

Take the Rue de Laeken to your left, then take the first road on your right, the Rue du Grand Hospice. Cross the square and keep walking straight on. Stop when you reach the Quai aux Briques and the Quai au Bois à Brûler.

7

Jaunes : Le transfert slave, BUCQUOY - TITO

To your left, you will be able to see Sainte-Catherine's Church. This building was designed by the architect Poelaert in 1854 and it dominates the ancient quays and Marché aux Poissons (the Fish Market). When they were built, each quay was designated for specific goods, a fact that is clear from the avenues' present names: le Quai aux Briques and the Quai au Bois à Brûler. In 1882, this commercial area was partly filled in. The new Marché aux Poissons replaced it and the Market survived until 1952. The present fish restaurants and oyster-sellers of the area are reminiscent of this maritime tradition.

In *Le Transfert Slave (The Czech Exchange)*, Daniel Jaunes, a sacked police inspector, is called by the head of the Secret Service (BSR) to conduct a special enquiry. In order to get to the police station, he goes along the quays of the Fish Market. These are accurately depicted. In order to carry out his

orders, Daniel Jaunes has to pretend to be Karol Shaumski, the President of the Czechoslovak Youth Union, because the Czech and he bear a strong resemblance to one another. Consequently, Jaunes has to go to the Brussels University and give a series of lectures on Marxism and Leninism. Shaumski intends to use the opportunity to apply for political asylum in Belgium. Finally, Daniel Jaunes as Shaumski is taken away to Prague and locked up by the Czech authorities who are convinced that he is their compatriot. Daniel manages to get back to Brussels by train with the help of Karol Chaumski's father.

JAN BUCQUOY
[1945]

Bucquoy the scriptwriter, wrote a novel and several plays before embarking on a career in comic strips. In 1980, he completed the *Jaunes* series with Tito, followed three years later by *Les Aventures de Gérard Craan*, in collaboration with Jacques Santi. He deals with sensitive subjects such as fascism and terrorism through his comic scripts.

TITO
[1957]

Tito, the artist and scriptwriter, studied graphic arts in France. In 1980, he designed the *Jaunes* series, based on a script by Bucquoy. He pursued his career with the *Solidad* and *Virginie* comic strips. Tito is a realist in his work who uses photographs in a documentary manner. Nowadays he writes his own storylines for comic strips.

The fountain is embellished with a bronze statue of Saint Michel and is 20 metres high. Initially, the fountain had pride of place in the centre of the Place De Brouckère (see also stage 15 with two further illustrations). Eventually, because the monument impeded the traffic on this arterial route, it was removed and installed on the Quai aux Briques, next to the Place Sainte-Catherine.

The plot of *Couleur Café (Coffee Colour)* is set in the 19th Century in the world of the commercial bourgeoisie that conducted business with the Belgian Congo. The hero, Lloyd, is an enigmatic dandy who is attempting to stop arms-trafficking. We see him in front of the fountain when it was still in the Place de Brouckère. The square can just be seen in the background.

PHILIPPE BERTHET
[1956]

Philippe Berthet, the comic scriptwriter and artist, had his first comic strips published in 1978 in a collaborative work *Le 9ème Rêve (The Ninth Dream)* which brought together the final-year work of the students of the Institut Saint-Luc in Brussels. His work made an appearance that was noted in the Spirou magazine, in which he designed Couleur Café, based on a storyline by Antoine Andrieu in 1980.

ANTOINE ANDRIEU
[1954]

As a storyline writer, Antoine Andrieu is mainly known for his *Couleur Café* story. In 1983, he created another storyline for *Le Journal Illustré*. It appeared in book form a year later, published by *Ice Crim's*.

Couleur Café, Philippe BERTHET

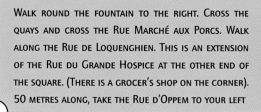

WALK ROUND THE FOUNTAIN TO THE RIGHT. CROSS THE QUAYS AND CROSS THE RUE MARCHÉ AUX PORCS. WALK ALONG THE RUE DE LOQUENGHIEN. THIS IS AN EXTENSION OF THE RUE DU GRANDE HOSPICE AT THE OTHER END OF THE SQUARE. (THERE IS A GROCER'S SHOP ON THE CORNER). 50 METRES ALONG, TAKE THE RUE D'OPPEM TO YOUR LEFT

9

On your right, you can see the *Billy the Cat* mural by Colman and Desberg. This adventure tells us of a small boy's life when he has become a kitten after dying in an accident. He is sent back to earth in feline form as a punishment for his past naughtiness. However, as he resigns himself to his new life, he discovers that his younger sister is being threatened by thugs. He does everything he can to help her. This mural shows Billy the Cat running around through the streets of Brussels.

STEPHEN DESBERG
[1954]

Stephen Desberg started out as a story-line writer as the assistant to Maurice Tillieux, working on several of the *Tif et Tondu* books. He then worked on numerous series for Dupuis along with artists Will, Maltaite, Desorgher and Colman, among others. In 1992, Desberg wrote the story for the first *La Vache* adventures. This book, produced by Casterman, was printed in Angoulême. Stephen Desberg also wrote *La 27ème lettre* and *Le Jardin des désirs* with Will, *L'étoile du désert* and *Le Scorpion* with Marini, *Tosca* with Vallès, *Les immortels* for Reculé etc.

STÉPHANE COLMAN
[1961]

The artist, Stéphane Colman drew Billy the Cat's first adventures to a storyline by Stephen Desberg in 1979 for the *Spirou* comic. In 1990, the Billy the Cat stories were published in book-form by Éditions Dupuis. Stéphane Colman also put his name to *White le choc!* In 1983 and Radical Café in 1984, both published by Éditions Magic Strip.

COLMAN - DESBERG © DUPUIS / PHOTO © DANIEL FOUSS, CBBD

Keep walking along the Rue d'Oppem. At the end of the road, take the Rue de Flandre on your left. Stop at the traffic lights.

Behind you, in the Rue de Flandre, you will see the Cubitus mural by Dupa.

Cubitus has taken the place of Manneken-Pis in his alcove in the Rue de l'Étuve. Maneken-Pis himself is playing the part of a tourist and looks confused as he observes the scene.

DUPA
[1945-2000]

Dupa, the artist and comic scriptwriter, was the assistant of Greg, the creator of *Achille Talon*. Consequently, Dupa was greatly inspired by Greg's work. Cubitus first appeared in 1968 in the *Tintin* comic, published by Éditions Lombard.

CROSS THE RUE MARCHÉ AUX PORCS AND KEEP WALKING
ALONG THE RUE DE FLANDRE WITH THE CUBITUS MURAL
BEHIND YOU. TAKE THE RUE PAYS DE LIÈGE (THE FIRST ON
THE LEFT) WHICH WILL LEAD YOU BACK TO THE QUAYS.
WALK TOWARDS ST. CATHERINE'S CHURCH ON YOUR
RIGHT.

11

You will find yourself in the heart of the old Marché aux Poissons (the Fish Market). On your right, before you reach the Church, you will see the 'Rugbyman 1' and '2' and 'François' restaurants.

In *De Zwarte Toren (The Black Tower)*, we see Van Zwam, the detective, looking for Nero in the Marché aux Poissons. During a walk through the city, Nero notices a beautiful young blond woman. He follows her and is knocked unconscious near the Tour Noire, behind St. Catherine's Church (see the next stopping-point). Nero's family, friends, the detective and Ricardo the burglar, all start searching for him. After many adventures, Nero's son finds him in a secret room inside the Tower.

This illustration conveys the atmosphere of the area well, but the scene is simplified. For example, it does not show the two other buildings between the two 'Rugbyman' restaurants. Marc Sleen slips in a touch of humour as well, by drawing an arrow saying 'Rugbyman 3,4,5,6 etc.' above the second restaurant in the picture.

De avonturen van Nero : De zwarte toren, Marc SLEEN

L'ÉTAT MORBIDE, LA MAISON-DIEU – HULET © 1987 – ÉDITIONS GLÉNAT

Go round the right-hand side of the Church. You will then reach the Place Sainte-Catherine.

(12)

From the square, you will be able to see the main façade of the Sainte-Catherine Church, and to the right of it, the tower. This is the only remaining part of the ancient church, and it backs onto the city ramparts.

L'État morbide - Acte Premier : La Maison-Dieu, Daniel HULET

L'État Morbide (The Morbid State) trilogy is set in the Sainte-Catherine area. The hero, Charles Haegeman, a young punk comic strip artist, takes possession of a flat whose previous tenant has died in mysterious circumstances. In the end, the flat gradually takes possession of Haegeman. More and more frightening events take place, illustrated by the use of dark and sombre colours in the work. Daniel Hulet takes us on a descent to hell towards the land of ghosts, right in the middle of the modern city. We should take note of the great accuracy with which the buildings and their surroundings in the area are depicted.

© 1987 – EDITIONS GLÉNAT

DANIEL HULET
[1947]

As an artist and scriptwriter, Daniel Hulet started in advertising before turning to comic strips. He created *Charabia* in a humorous style, for the *Tintin* comic, before adopting a more realistic approach. In 1987, Daniel Hulet designed the first part of *L'État Morbide* in three volumes based on his own storylines for the publishers Éditions Glénat. His talent was recognised as a result of the *Pharaon* and *Les Chemins de la Gloire (The Roads to Glory)* series.

TAKE THE ROAD THAT RUNS ALONGSIDE THE CHURCH, TO THE LEFT-HAND SIDE OF THE TOWER.
YOU WILL EMERGE FROM THE OTHER SIDE OF THE PLACE SAINTE-CATHERINE.

13

On your right you will see the Tour Noire (Black Tower), surrounded, sadly, by the walls of the Novotel. The Tower forms part of the original city walls that were constructed in the 13th Century.

De avonturen van Nero : De zwarte toren, Marc SLEEN

This illustration shows the Black Tower, and, on the right, Petoetje and Petatje running away. The mysterious blond woman who Nero had fallen for is also in the strip.

In this introductory illustration to the story, the hero, Charles Haegeman, arrives in the Sainte-Catherine area where he notices a flat for rent. The colours that are used for this view of the Church immediately convey the frightening atmosphere that Daniel Hulet wishes to achieve.

L'État morbide - Acte Premier : La Maison-Dieu, Daniel HULET

Walk across the square and keep walking as far as the traffic lights. Cross the Rue de la Vierge Noire and take the Rue de l'Évêque towards the Centre Monnaie (the Monnaie shopping centre). At the crossroads 100 metres further on, turn left into the Boulevard Anspach. Stop at the next set of traffic lights.

(15)

© 2004 – LOUIS JOOS

You are arriving in the Place de Brouckère. This square is frequently depicted in comic strips.

Monsieur Lambart, the hero of Ostende-Miami, lives in the centre of Brussels. He goes through the Place de Brouckère on his way home and then gets ready to go to a jazz concert at the casino in Ostende, given by his favourite jazz singer. From there, a series of unexpected events takes him all the way to Miami. In this story, the De Brouckère square is repre-sented as it was in the 1950s, complete with the Anspach fountain (now situated on the Quai aux Briques). In the illustration we can see that

Ostende-Miami, JOOS - ANDRIEU

various changes have been made since that time: the square in the centre was surrounded by the lamp standards; it served as a pedestrian and parking area and there are trams running round the square..... Equally worthy of note are the unencumbered views of the main roads on both sides of the Anspach fountain (to the left, Boulevard Émile Jacqmain and to the right, Boulevard Adolphe Max). Nowadays the views are obstructed by office blocks of the northern part of the city and the Sheraton Hotel. The Coca-Cola sign was already in place, however, in the 1950s.

LOUIS JOOS
[1940]

Louis Joos, the comic strip artist and storyline writer, published his first book, *Colaxa*, in 1982 with the publisher Futuropolis. *Ostende-Miami*, one of Andrieu's storylines, was initially completed for a Belgian magazine before being published in 1984 in book form. Although he is a black-and-white illustration specialist, Louis Joos does produce work in colour for children's books. He also teaches the art of comic strips and illustration and the Boitsfort Academy in Brussels.

MALIK
[1948]

The artist and storyline writer Malik published stories in *Tintin* and *Spirou* having studied at the Académie des Beaux-Arts in Brussels. At the same time, he illustrated humorous work such as *Le Plombier* and *Cupidon*. In 1996, Malik illustrated *Gertrude aux Pays des Belges* by Stéphane Steeman.

STÉPHANE STEEMAN
[1933]

The humorous writer, Stéphane Steeman, is passionate about comic strips. He is currently the President of *Les Amis d'Hergé*. He enjoys making fun of Belgian eccentricities such as people's linguistic and political problems. In *Gertrude aux Pays des Belges*, he conveys various opinions, dealing mainly with Brussels town-planning problems, through Gertrude. She is a character who Stéphane Steeman created twenty-five years ago and is a personality who many can identify with. Gertrude featured in the *Revue des Galeries* between 1982 and 1992 and appeared in the 'Bon week-end' RTBF (French-speaking Belgian Radio & TV) programme from 1992 to 1998.

In *Gertrude au Pays des Belges (Gertrude in Belgium)*, Stéphane Steeman expresses his love for the old Brussels and its environment through the nostalgic comic strips. He goes even further back in time than Louis Joos, since the Coca-Cola advertising sign has not yet appeared on the main building in the square. He also reveals to us the splendour of that building which at that time had a statue on its roof. The statue was replaced more than fifty years later by the symbol of Americanisation, the Coca-Cola sign.

Gertrude au pays des Belges, STEEMAN - MALIK

Bubbly Brussels provides evidence of the extent of the traffic in the Place de Brouckère. In the majority of the illustrations, the 'Métropole' is the main feature: this legendary hotel has existed for more than a century and has been patronised by numerous comic strip characters.

In *Snake* the two heroes, Bob Morane and his friend Bill actually stay at the hotel. Bob Morane is conducting an enquiry into the Bénédicité Snake affair. She is a young Haïtian woman who wears a snake round her neck. Several people die as a result of being bitten by it. In the background in the illustration, to the right of the Métropole Hotel, the Tour Monnaie is visible. This building houses the administrative services of the Brussels City Council.

Barelli's Adventures: Bubbly Brussels, Bob DE MOOR

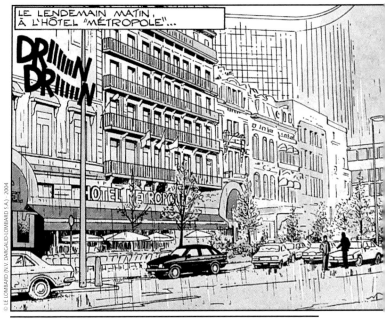

Une aventure de Bob Morane : Snake, CORIA - VERNES

CORIA
[1948]

The comic strip artist Coria, who is Spanish by birth, moved to Belgium after he met the sister of the designer William Vance. Coria worked as assistant on the designs of various books such as *Bob Morane*. In 1979, the scriptwriter Henri Vernes and William Vance entrusted him with the completion of entire comic strip designs. This recent collaborative work has led to more than thirty books of Bob Morane adventures.

9. CROSS THE BOULEVARD ANSPACH (TO YOUR RIGHT). GO STRAIGHT ALONG THE RUE FOSSÉ-AUX-LOUPS (DIRECTLY AHEAD OF YOU). NEXT, TAKE THE FIRST ROAD ON THE RIGHT. YOU WILL THEN SEE THE THÉÂTRE DE LA MONNAIE (MONNAIE THEATRE) WHEN YOU REACH THE PLACE DE LA MONNAIE.

16

This theatre, built in the neo-classical style, was the work of Louis Damesme (1817). After a major fire, it was re-built by Joseph Poelaert in 1856. In 1985, the roof of the theatre was raised by four metres, mainly for accoustic reasons.

Le Code Zimmerman, l'Opéra de la mort, CARIN - RIVIÈRE - BORILE

In volume one of *Le Code Zimmerman, l'Opéra de la Mort (The Zimmerman Code, the Opera of Death)*, Victor Sackville is one of King George V's agents. He is travelling round Europe in 1916 at the time when pressure from the Germans is becoming increasingly noticeable. He mingles with the journalists and makes use of his relationships with the aristocracy in order to carry out the secret missions that he is charged with. The main focus of the action is the theatre, and it is represented in the context of its era, the First World War. In the illustration

there are signs of the German occupation and the splendid details of the building are depicted meticulously. We can see the lamp standards of the period, the buildings to the left of the theatre that have now been replaced, as well as the cars with access right up to the front of the building.

Au Dolle Mol is one of *Gérard Craan's* adventures. It is a fictional-political comic strip: the violent and imaginary action takes place in a Europe at the end of the 19ᵗʰ Century when the political map is being entirely re-drawn. *Gérard Craan* belongs to a group of anarchists and the Monnaie Theatre is used as a decorative element: *Gérard Craan* walks in

Une aventure de Gérard Craan : Au Dolle Mol, SANTI - BUCQUOY

front of the building when he has left the 'Dolle Mol'. This is one of the restaurants on the Rue des Éperonniers where he had to meet a secret agent during the course of his work, before finally going to a reception on the Rue Fossé-aux-Loups. The Monnaie Theatre remains very realistic, in spite of some embellishments like curtains at the windows...

© BOB DE MOOR - 2004

Barelli's Adventures: Bubbly Brussels, Bob DE MOOR

In *Bubbly Brussels* Barelli watches the thief who has stolen his script as Hudebert Whitloaf is just about to fall off the roof of the Monnaie Theatre. The comic strip provides us with a contemporary view of the theatre as well as an extremely detailed view of the building's pediment.

JACQUES SANTI
[1960]

Santi, a comic strip artist, Santi has worked on numerous storylines by Bucquoy such as *Les Aventures de Gérard Kraan (The Adventures of Gérard Kraan)* and *Chroniques de Fin de Siècle (Late 19th Century Chronicles)* between 1985 and 1988.

FRANÇOIS RIVIÈRE
[1949]

The storyline writer, journalist and novelist, François Rivière, edited his first work that was for *l'École d'Hergé (Hergé's School)* in 1976. In 1981, he wrote the *Thierry Laudacieux* story that was drawn by Alain Goffin for a monthly comic. Two years later, he worked as co-writer on *Le Privé d'Hollywood*, drawn by Philippe Berthet. François Rivière worked with Gabrielle Borile to create storylines for the *Victor Sackville* series. He also writes numerous novels, literary reviews, essays and biographies.

FRANCIS CARIN
[1950]

Francis Carin, the comic strip artist, worked collaboratively on the preparation of *Spirou* and *Tintin* comics in the mid-1970s. During the same period, he drew several complete stories for *Tintin*. In 1983, he started working on the *Victor Sackville* series in collaboration with François Rivière and Gabrielle Borile for the storyline.

GABRIELLE BORILE
[1953]

Gabrielle Borile, the storyline writer, has a degree in Journalism. At first she worked as a translator before travelling the world as a reporter. In 1983, she co-wrote the adventures of *Victor Sackville*. She also wrote the *Alex Nora* series with Chantal Heuvel in 1991 and the storylines for *Lanterna Magica* two years later.

10. WALK ACROSS THE PLACE DE LA MONNAIE TO THE RIGHT OF THE THEATRE. WHEN YOU REACH THE TRAFFIC LIGHTS, CROSS THE ROAD AND TAKE THE RUE DES FRIPIERS. (USE THE ANSPACH CENTRE – MEGASTORE ON THE CORNER ON THE RIGHT AS A LANDMARK. TURN DOWN THE SECOND ROAD ON THE LEFT: THE RUE MARCHÉ AUX HERBES.

There is an illustration of the Rue Marché aux Herbes below.

Charly, Le Tueur, MAGDA - LAPIÈRE

Our hero, Charly, is an eight year-old boy who is the victim of violent nightmares. He dreams about people who kill themselves and accuse him of being responsible for their deaths. However, while watching the TV news, his mother and he realise that his nightmares are in fact real. His mother decides therefore to take action and to take herself to Brussels to face the killer.

The city is the backdrop for this story. The illustration of the Rue Marché aux Herbes is an accurate depiction of the real street. However, note that since the book was published in 1997, Christiaensen has been replaced by another toyshop.

MAGDA
[1956]

Magda Seron, the comic strip artist, joined the Édouard Aidans studios in 1977 where she created *Tumak* for the daily paper *Vers l'Avenir*. In her detailed style she has illustrated various deeply human stories for comics such as *Tremplin* and *Spirou*. Magda drew *Charly*, the strange little boy, for *Spirou*, based on a storyline by Denis Lapière.

DENIS LAPIÈRE
[1958]

The storyline writer, Denis Lapière, is a Sociology graduate. He opened a specialised comic bookshop in Charleroi and this inspired him to write several plots himself. In 1989, he created *Alice et Leopold* with Olivier Wozniak for the *Spirou* comic. In this series, he writes about African and European co-habitation in the colonised Belgian Congo of the 1920s. In 1990, Denis Lapière wrote the storyline for *Charly*, completing *Tif et Tondu* a year later. He also wrote *La Race des Seigneurs* and *Luka* in 1995 and 1996 respectively.

(18)

Imagine Michel Vaillant and the police officers engaging in a car-chase in the tiny streets of the historic centre of Brussels...

Michel Vaillant and his friends Steve Warson and Julie Wood go to the Amigo hotel in Brussels for the gala opening of the Racing Show. They are greeted there by Thierry Boutsen and also meet a former pilot, Bob Cramer. However, Julie Wood is kidnapped in a

Michel Vaillant : Racing-Show, Jean GRATON

red Mercedes, driven by Cramer. The Mercedes is involved in a car chase with the Brussels police up at the Palais de Justice (The Law Courts). They race down the Rue de Régence, cross the Sablon and continue into the Rue du Lombard. Meanwhile, Michel Vaillant goes to the Police Station to ask for news of his friend Julie. As he leaves the building, he sees the Mercedes roaring past on the way to the Boulevard Anspach. In his Vaillante car, Michel Vaillant catches up

Michel Vaillant : Racing-Show, Jean GRATON

with the Mercedes when it is level with the Bourse and continues the car-chase through the tiny streets of the historic centre of Brussels (the Petite Rue des Bouchers). Michel Vaillant and the police officers end up stopping the Mercedes in the Grand-Place. In this comic strip Brussels is the scene of the action and is shown in great detail.

JEAN GRATON
[1923]

Jean Graton, the comic strip artist and storyline writer, is French. He was born in Nantes and his father, a steward at the Nantes Motorcycling Club, took him to the Le Mans 24-hour race when he was very young. Events forced him to manage on his own very early in life, and at sixteen Jean Graton went to work in the shipyards.

The work was very demanding and in 1947, Graton left Nantes for Brussels with the idea of living by his talent: drawing. He sold a few drawings for advertising and worked on the *Les Sports* newspaper while taking a course in advertising. It was by chance that one Friday, 13th, he went into the World Press Agency where Jean-Michel Charlier entrusted Jean Graton with completing the first *Oncle Paul* strips. After some complete stories in the *Spirou* and *Tintin* comics, Graton drew on his detailed knowledge of motor sport and created the Michael Vaillant character (1959). Nowadays, the Michael Vaillant exploits fill more than sixty-five books, a TV serial, sixty-five episodes of animated cartoons and a film that was written and produced by Luc Besson. Jean Graton's son Philippe, involved at the beginning of these recent projects, writes storylines for the new books in a series that has already sold more than twenty million copies.

In the middle of the Petite Rue des Bouchers, between numbers 21 and 23, on the right-hand side, there is the Impasse Schuddeveld. At the end of it you will find the Toone theatre and tavern.

19

This puppet theatre for adults opened in 1830. It presents well-known classical plays that have been adapted into Bruxellois (the Brussels dialect) and they are full of expressions that are typical of, and still used by certain inhabitants of the Marolles area of the city. For more than a hundred and fifty years, the tradition has been passed down from generation to generation in spite of the many changes to the location of the theatre, as well as successive buy-outs of the business. The theatre has also survived urban development and the removal of slums in the city. As far as the tavern is concerned, you can try the Belgian beers there in a traditional rustic atmosphere.

Ric Hochet : Les témoins de Satan, TIBET - A.P. DUCHÂTEAU

In this Ric Hochet adventure, Gérald is assassinated on his uncle's property. Inspector Bourdon suspects Lucia Demal, Gérald's girlfriend, of the crime. Ric Hochet is sent on a mission to Brussels to conduct his own enquiry. Maître Brunet, a famous lawyer, also goes to the capital to defend Lucia's case. Ric Hochet receives a phone call inviting him to go to the Toon theatre and he is attacked and injured there. During the trial, Maître Brunet manages to prove Lucia innocent, but Ric Hochet pusues his own enquiry and finds that she is guilty.

AT THE END OF THE PETITE RUE DES BOUCHERS, WALK ALONG THE RUE DES BOUCHERS TO YOUR RIGHT. APPROXIMATELY 200 METRES ALONG THERE, YOU WILL FIND YOURSELF IN THE MIDDLE OF THE GALERIES SAINT-HUBERT. TURN RIGHT INTO THE GALERIE DE LA REINE.

20

Le Code Zimmerman, l'Opéra de la mort, CARIN - RIVIÈRE - BORILE

These arcades of shops, the first of their type in Europe, were designed by the architect Jean-Pierre Cluysenaar. They were built in 1847 in a neo-classical style and comprise the Galerie du Roi, the Galerie de la Reine and the Galerie des Princes.

In *Le Code Zimmermann* and *Bubbly Brussels* stories, the arcades form the backdrop to the stories. Both the books show the hero, Victor Sackville, face-on, and Barelli and his aunt from behind, walking through the Galeries Saint-Hubert.

Barelli's Adventures: Bubbly Brussels, Bob DE MOOR

Les aventures d'Hergé, STANISLAS - BOCQUET - FROMENTAL

In *Les Aventures d'Hergé (The Hergé Adventures)*, the arcades form an integral part of the story. Notice, too, that the Théâtre royal des Galeries is advertising a performance of an adaptation of *Tintin aux Indes (Tintin in the Indies)* and *Mystère du Diamant bleu (The Blue Diamond Mystery)*. *Le Code Zimmerman* is set during the First World War, whereas the German soldiers in the background of the illustration of *Les Aventures d'Hergé* clearly place the story in the Second World War.

There is a clear difference in context between *Bubbly Brussels* and the two previously mentioned stories. Also, as it is peacetime in *Bubbly Brussels*, we can see the European flags on both sides of the arcade.

JOSÉ-LOUIS BOCQUET
[1962]

José-Louis Bocquet, a storyline writer and editor, has completed several anthologies, such as *Les premières années de la bande dessinées*. Amongst his comic strip stories we find *Le privé d'Hollywood*, drawn by Philippe Berthet in 1983, and the *Dorian Dombre* trilogy which was drawn by Francis Vallès in 1989.

Ric Hochet : Les témoins de Satan, TIBET - A.P. DUCHÂTEAU

In *Les Témoins de Satan (Satan's Witnesses)*, Ric Hochet chases his attacker through the Galeries royales on a motorbike after shots have been fired in the Grand-Place. Here, the emphasis is on the action and not on the architecture, yet the details like those of the cutlery-shop on the left, are realistic.

JEAN-LUC FROMENTAL
[1950]

Storyline writer, journalist and novelist, Jean-Luc Fromentier became a comic script critic in 1980 on the *Matin de Paris* newspaper. He has worked in advertising, television and on comic strips and created several comic strip anthologies. He has also written the storylines for 26 short animated cartoons for French TV.

STANISLAS
[1961]

The artist Stanislas is an interior designer by training. He started working on comic strips in 1984. Having drawn for numerous publications, he created the *Victor Lavallois* series with Laurent Rullier. In 1996, he worked on a comic strip adaptation of Hergé's life.

You will be able to see the Grand-Place from the Rue de la Colline.

The illustration below shows the beginning of the motorbike chase between Ric Hochet and his assailant. Tibet is very faithful to real-life in his depiction of the scene of the action here.

Ric Hochet : Les témoins de Satan, TIBET - A.P. DUCHÂTEAU

KEEP WALKING AND YOU WILL BE IN THE GRAND-PLACE
(THE MAIN SQUARE IN BRUSSELS).

22

Michel Vaillant : Racing-Show, Jean GRATON

At the time of the attack on Brussels in 1695 by French troops under Maréchal de Vileroi, more than four thousand buildings in the centre of Brussels were damaged or burnt down. With the exception of the tower of the Hôtel de Ville, the entirety of the Grand-Place was in ruins. It was rebuilt over the next five years in an even more sumptuous style than it had been before 1695. In order to rebuild the Guild houses, Italian Renaissance and current Parisian-style features were added. Wooden buildings gave way to curved gable-ends that were heavily adorned with columns, bas-reliefs and medallions. Substantial amounts of gilding were used on the facades in order to give prominence to the various trades' Guild houses.

Manneken-Pis, l'irascible (Bad-tempered Manneken-Pis) shows us the Grand-Place in its lively, traditional guise. Spike and Suzy go there to see the centre of Brussels. After passing the Manneken-Pis, Suzy realises that she has lost her doll, Muffin. She retraces her steps and sees a van on the point of driving over the doll. However, at that moment, Manneken-Pis 'waters' the van's windscreen, and the driver, who is distracted by the action, crashes the van into a wall. From that moment, after saving Muffin, Manneken-Pis follows Spike and Suzy in their adventures.

Bob et Bobette : Manneken-Pis, l'irascible, Willy VANDERSTEEN

In Michel Vaillant, the architectural details of the Grand-Place are completely accurate.

Michel Vaillant : Racing-Show, Jean GRATON

The Grand-Place is where the great car-chase ends.

TAKE THE RUE CHARLES BULS, IMMEDIATELY TO THE LEFT OF THE HÔTEL DE VILLE. THIS ROAD BECOMES THE RUE DE L'ÉTUVE.

23

In *Le Fantôme espagnol (The Spanish Ghost)*, Willy Vandersteen shows the tower of the Hôtel de Ville, presided over by St. Michael bringing down the dragon. In this adventure, Spike, Suzy and Ambrose find themselves in a Brueghel painting, living through the events of the era,

accompanied by the Spanish ghost that they have met in the museum. This is why they are shown wearing period clothes.

Bob et Bobette : Le Fantôme espagnol, Willy VANDERSTEEN

Michel Vaillant : Racing-Show, Jean GRATON

You are walking past the Amigo hotel where Ric Hochet and Michel Vaillant 'stayed' in the story.

Ric Hochet : Les témoins de Satan, TIBET - A.P. DUCHÂTEAU

CROSS THE ROAD AT THE LIGHTS AND KEEP WALKING ALONG THE RUE DE L'ÉTUVE. ON YOUR RIGHT, AT NUMBERS 40-45, YOU WILL FIND ANOTHER SHOP WHICH SELLS TINTIN GOODS. STOP AT THE NEXT CORNER.

(24)

To your left, Manneken-Pis is waiting for you. He is the little character who symbolises Brussels. This small bronze statue dates from the beginning of the 18th Century and is the work of Jérôme Duquesnoy. According to the legend, this three year-old boy got lost and was found five days later in the process of producing a 'clear jet of water' at the corner of the Rue de l'Étuve and the Rue du Chêne. Another story tells of how Manneken-Pis put out the great fire of the same era in Brussels in the same way.

De avonturen van Nero : De zwarte toren, Marc SLEEN

In *De zwarte toren (The Black Tower)*, Mark Sleen introduces his hero, Nero, who discovers the Manneken-Pis statue while walking round the centre of Brussels, before he is locked up in the Black Tower.

Bob et Bobette : Manneken-Pis, l'irascible, Willy VANDERSTEEN

In this illustration from *Spike and Suzy*, our three heroes mingle with the tourists in front of the statue of Manneken-Pis.

TAKE THE RUE DES GRANDS CARMES (ON YOUR RIGHT, OPPOSITE THE MANNEKEN-PIS STATUE). CROSS THE RUE DU MIDI AND KEEP WALKING. AT THE END OF THE RUE DES GRANDS CARMES, TURN RIGHT INTO THE RUE DU MARCHÉ AU CHARBON. STOP AT THE NEXT CROSSROADS.

(25)

Here you can enjoy the Frank Pé mural that represents *Broussaille* and his girlfriend crossing the Plattesteen, and this is exactly where you are. There is an amusing little detail here: at the top of the mural you can see an illustration of the mural itself.

FRANK PÉ © DUPUIS / PHOTO : © DANIEL FOUSS, CBBD

FRANK PÉ
[1956]

The artist Frank Pé created the character of Broussaille, the nature-lover, for the *Spirou* comic in 1978. He takes us through his simple adventures where marvel and fantasy play a special role. Frank Pé has been honoured with many prizes for his book *Les Baleines publiques (The Public Whales)*. He has also worked on full-length cartoon films.

At the same crossroads, behind you in the Rue au Marché au Charbon, you will see the mural by Francis Carin. This represents a scene from *L'Opéra de la Mort*, the first volume of the *Le Code Zimmerman*. Here you can see Victor Sackville walking down the Marché au Charbon. In the mural there is also the façade of a house that is situated at the corner of the Rue des Grands Carmes which you have just left. You can also see the bell-tower of the Bon-Secours Church.

TURN TOWARDS THE *B*ROUSSAILLE MURAL BY **F**RANK **P**É IN THE **M**ARCHÉ AU **C**HARBON. **C**ROSS THE **R**UE DU **M**IDI AND CONTINUE WALKING TOWARDS THE **P**OLICE **S**TATION.

(27)

Michel Vaillant : Racing-Show, Jean GRATON

Here is an illustration that shows the Rue du Marché au Charbon with the Police Station on the right. This is where Michel Vaillant went, and on the left the bare wall

FRANÇOIS SCHUITEN
[1956]

François Schuiten, the storyline writer and artist, has been working since 1981 with Benoît Peeters on the *Cités obscures (Obscure cities)* series. He creates his own coherent and utopian world and is clearly inspired by the illustrators and architects of the beginning of the 20th Century. The essential characteristics of his work are the partial buildings and plunging perspectives in a somewhat inhuman landscape. Since 1991, he has worked on a project to adapt *Les Cités obscures* for film.

on which we can now see François Schuiten's mural, *Le Passage (The Passage)*. In the middle of the breathtaking perspectives of the buildings in the mural you can see the bell-tower of the Saint-Jacques-sur-Coudenberg Church, situated in the Place Royale.

Opposite you there is the Maison du Roi. On the first floor, you will find the 'Bruxelles à ciel ouvert' exhibition. This display demonstrates the evolution of urban development in the city (known as the 'Pentagon') over the last thousand years.

Gord is a futuristic comic strip that offers an apocalyptic vision of Brussels. The entire city is shown under water, abandoned, and covered in wild vegetation. Only the main monuments can be seen in the ruined city. The hero, Gord, is disorientated in this hostile world and he meets Angus Van Cleef, nicknamed 'Le spit du snack'.

CHRISTIAN DENAYER
[1945]

Artist and storyline writer Christian Denayer, worked as Jean Graton's assistant on *Michel Vaillant*, and Tibet's on *Ric Hochet*. At the same time, he created *Yalek* and *Alain Chevalier* based on a storyline by A-P Duchâteau, in addition to a series called *Les Casseurs*. In 1987, with Franz as scriptwriter, he completed *Gord*. From 2000 he worked on this work , returning to comic strip adventures in 2001 with *Wayne Shelton*, one of Jean Van Hamme's scripts.

FRANZ
[1948-2003]

The scriptwriter and artist Franz really started work on comic strips in 1969 in the *Spirou* and *Tintin* comics. He created historical work on Brussels and Belgium. From 1979, he developed his own characters such as Leister Cockney. Franz's work is characterised by his gift for graphics and an extraordinary imagination. In 1987, he created the *Gord* comic strip with Christian Denayer, published by Éditions du Lombard.

Gord, Le spit du Snack, FRANZ - DENAYER

Angus helps Gord in his mission by taking him in his Spitfire and bombarding the buildings where his enemies are in hiding. Below, Denayer shows Gord and his girlfriend Abla watching the 'Spit du snack's Spitfire flying in front of the spire of the Maison du Roi. Although the artist presents us with a futuristic and apocalyptic vision of the city, the views of the buildings that are illustrated are realistic.

Below, there are two views of the Grand-Place looking onto the Rue au Beurre. Magda and Tibet depict Brussels in an accurate way.

Charly, Le Tueur, MAGDA - LAPIÈRE

Ric Hochet : Les témoins de Satan, TIBET - A.P. DUCHÂTEAU

BARLY BARUTI
[1959]

The comic strip artist Barli Baruti started doing animations in the graphic studios of his native country, the Democratic Republic of Congo. He has worked in the Hergé Studios. In *Eva K,* especially, he developed a theme of opposition to dictatorship.

FOLLOW THE RUE AU BEURRE WHICH IS TO YOUR LEFT, AT THE FAR END OF THE GRAND-PLACE, AS FAR AS THE BOURSE (STOCK EXCHANGE). SAINT-NICHOLAS CHURCH, ON YOUR RIGHT, IS SURROUNDED BY SMALL HOUSES. TAKE THE RUE DE LA BOURSE. THIS RUNS ALONG THE RIGHT-HAND SIDE OF THE BOURSE. HERE YOU CAN SEE SOME RUINS OF THE FOUNDATIONS OF BRUSSELS. STOP AT THE BOULEVARD D'ANSPACH.

30

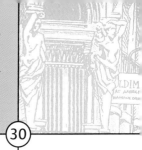

On your right, a view of the Place De Brouckère comes into view at the end of the Boulevard Anspach.

The book *Objectif Terre (Objective: Earth)* was created in collaboration with the General Administration for Co-operative Development and Greenpeace. The book's main aim is to make the reader aware of environmental problems. The two heroes, Sako and Yannick, live in Africa. They enter a school competition that is organised by the World Wildlife Fund, and win a trip for a month to Europe, with children from all over the world. In this comic strip story, Brussels is not very important; the city is just one of the European stopping-off points. The view towards the Place de Brouckère has been accurately depicted. Notice the difference in the view, compared with stage 15: here the Sheraton Hotel in the background is far larger.

Les aventures de Sako et Yannick : Objectif Terre, Barly BARUTI

31

Here are two views of the Bourse and the Boulevard Anspach. The Bourse, which was built in1868, was designed by the architect Léon Suys as the jewel in the crown of the newly constructed boulevards. The building is decorated with architectural ornamentation such as pilasters, columns, friezes and sculpted pediments. These sculptures convey the themes of Belgium, industry, commerce and land and sea transport, symbolising the stability of the country.

Jean Graton has drawn the car-chase between Bob Kramer's red Mercedes and Michel Vaillant's Vaillante in the Place de la Bourse as it now looks.

Michel Vaillant : Racing-Show, Jean GRATON

Des ombres sur le sable (Shadows on the Sand) is the sixth in the *Pharaon* series. Having accomplished his mission in Alaska, the hero, Pharaon, asks his boss, Cobra for a sabbatical break. He hides in a secret part of Brussels in order to kill himself. The black shadow discovers him and follows him round the city. The northern part of the city is covered in sand and pyramids rise up in the midst of the buildings. Pharaon walks along the Boulevard d'Anspach, the Place De Brouckère and in front of the Bourse. Seeing these buildings turning into sand, he hardly notices the traffic and is knocked down by a car in the Rue August Orts. In hospital, his clone attempts to take his place and other nightmarish hallucinations take Pharaon into new adventures in the country of sand and Egyptian tombs. In the illustration, Pharaon's hallucinations have not yet taken over. The Bourse is realistic, but the sand is beginning to cover the pavements and the underground station.

PEUT-ÊTRE LE CAUCHEMAR CONTINUAIT-IL ...

Pharaon : Des ombres sur le sable, DUCHÂTEAU - HULET

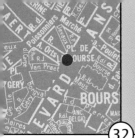

CROSS THE RUE PAUL DEVAUX AND STOP WHEN YOU REACH THE RUE AUGUSTE ORTS WHICH IS OPPOSITE THE BOURSE.

32

To your left you will have a different view of the Bourse with the tower of the Hôtel de Ville behind it, to the right.

In the *Des ombres sur le sable (The Shadows on the Sand)*, Pharaon's hallucinations have given him a unique view of the Brussels' buildings. In this illustration, he tries to cross the Rue Auguste Orts, completely engulfed in sand, while the Bourse and the tower of the Hôtel de Ville are being rapidly eroded and are sinking further and further into the sand.

Pharaon : Des ombres sur le sable, DUCHÂTEAU - HULET

WALK ALONG THE RUE AUGUSTE ORTS AND THE RUE
JULES VAN PRAET. STOP AT THE TRAFFIC LIGHTS AT
O'REILLY'S IRISH CAFÉ.

33

To your left, you can see another view of the Boulevard Anspach.

Le Code Zimmerman (The Zimmerman Code) offers us an illustration
of the Place de la Bourse in 1916. Once again, Francis Carin recreates
the impression of that era with trams, the newspaper seller....

Le Code Zimmerman, l'Opéra de la mort, CARIN - RIVIÈRE - BORILE

CROSS THE BOULEVARD ANSPACH AGAIN AND WALK ALONG THE RIGHT-HAND SIDE FOR ABOUT FIFTY METRES. ON YOUR LEFT, AT NUMBER 100 YOU WILL FIND THE 'BRÜSEL' BOOKSHOP AND GALLERY. THE DESIGN OF THE INTERIOR IS BASED ON OBSCURE CITIES BY SCHUITEN AND PEETERS. KEEP WALKING ALONG THE BOULEVARD ANSPACH AND CROSS THE RUE DES PIERRES.

(34)

The 'Ancienne Belgique' Concert Hall is to your left, at number 110.

Barelli's Adventures: Bubbly Brussels, Bob DE MOOR

In the illustration above, Barelli and his aunt are discussing the possible disappearance of the 'Ancienne Belgique'. Since the book was published, this enormous concert hall has been entirely renovated with the help of finance from the Flemish Community. Both international and local artistes perform here. Various concert rooms and facilities, as well as sizeable audiences, mean that the facility is well-used.

Continue walking along the Boulevard Anspach. At the next crossroads, on the Plattesteen, you will find two bookshop-galleries: at number 124 the 'Bulle d'Or', and at 126-8, 'Multi BD'. Keep walking along the boulevard, then cross the Rue des Teinturiers.

35

Les Cités obscures : Brüsel, SCHUITEN - PEETERS

© CASTERMAN

On your right, in this road at right-angles to the boulevard, you will see the two bell-towers of the Notre-Dame-des-Riches-Claires. They look down over the houses of the area. This 18th Century church is typical of the Brabant Baroque style.

Les Cités obscures (Obscure cities) series pays homage to the great architects of the recent centuries. Progress and science also play an important part in the books. In the Brüsel volume, the city of Brussels is a major element in the story. Developers and politicians set about changing the city without the slightest respect for the past. They start to demolish the areas that are human in scale. Brüsel, the obscure city, is built. A series of six adventures illustrates this depressing development.

In the illustration below from the first part of Le plastique c'est chic (Plastic is Chic) we meet Constant, a florist who walks through the small streets near the bell-towers of the Riches-Claires Church. Constant, after much hesitation, will convert his shop to selling plastic flowers that do not need attention or water.

BENOÎT PEETERS
[1956]

As a storywriter and novelist, Benoît Peeters has worked both in the media and in the world of comic strips. He has published various anthologies dedicated to Hergé's work, such as Le Monde d'Hergé and La Bibliothèque de Moulinsart. He has also published critical work such as Töppfer: l'invention de la BD. In 1982, he wrote the storylines for the Cités obscures series by François Schuiten, followed by Plagiat!, drawn by Alain Goffin. In 1996, he wrote Architectures Rêvées as a tribute to Victor Horta and his achievements. In October 2001 he completed the first film-version of L'Affaire Desombres, a veritable journey into Obscure cities.

On your left you will see the *Ric Hochet* mural by Tibet.

Inspector Bourdon is coming out of his house with his dog. He is surprised to see Ric Hochet hanging from the guttering. From the spot where he is standing, the Inspector cannot see the murderer going into the room on the first floor and so he does not understand why Ric Hochet is trying to get to the window. Tibet chose to lengthen the façade of the adjoining house in order as a setting for the action in the mural. This effect integrates the work completely into the Rue du Bon-Secours.

Go back to the Boulevard Anspach. This becomes the Boulevard Lemonnier as far as the Boulevard du Midi (5-10 minutes' walk). At the traffic lights, cross the Avenue Stalingrad at the lights on your left. Stop before you reach the Nord-Midi stations' railway bridge. The Gare du Midi (South Station) is on your right.

(37)

De Moor and Jacobs have both drawn the old Gare du Midi (see below).

In *Bubbly Brussels*, Barelli and his aunt go to the Gare du Midi on a Sunday, market day. The station is shown in the form it had until the beginning of the 1990s. It was completely redeveloped afterwards to accommodate the TGV (high-speed trains). Bob de Moor emphasises the multicultural aspect of the area around the station.

There is another representation of the old Gare du Midi in *The Mystery of the Great Pyramid*. This Blake and Mortimer story starts in Cairo, where the

The adventures of Blake and Mortimer : The Mystery of the Great Pyramid (part I), Edgar P. JACOBS

Barelli's Adventures: Bubbly Brussels, Bob DE MOOR

NEXT MORNING AT THE SOUTH STATION ... IT´S SUNDAY AND MARKET TIME AND THE PLACE IS CROWDED FROM THE BREAK OF DAY.

The train pulls in at 10 a.m. We've still got half an hour, auntie.

Time to buy some flowers for Anna.

© BOB DE MOOR - 2004

museum curator finds fragments of papyrus that might lead to the re-discovery of the funerary treasure of Akhnaton. The curator invites Professor Mortimer to help him de-code this papyrus. However, the treasure stirs up the greed of antiquities' traffickers like Olrik. Several events at the museum and at an antiquary's put Mortimer's life in danger. Mortimer asks for help from his friend at Scotland Yard, Captain Blake, after bungling the arrest of Olrik and losing the co-operation of the local police. This is how Blake finds himself getting on the Ostend ferry and finally taking the train for Brussels. At the Gare du Midi, Blake jumps into a taxi to go to the Métropole Hotel, where he stays, before going through various adventures at his next port of call, Athens.

EDGAR PIERRE JACOBS
[1904-1987]

The artist and comic strip writer E.P. Jacobs rapidly became passionate about drawing and music. From 1944, Hergé entrusted him with the colouring work of some of his books: *Tintin au Congo*, *Tintin en Amérique*, *Le temple du soleil* and *Les sept boules de crystal*. This collaboration led to a great friendship between the two men. In 1946, Hergé invited E.P. Jacobs to work with him on the launch of the *Tintin* comic. Over time, Jacobs wrote several adventures such as *The Mystery of the Great Pyramid*, *La Marque jaune*, *SOS météors*, etc.

AT THE END OF BOULEVARD JAMAR, TO YOUR RIGHT, YOU CAN SPOT THE ÉDITIONS LOMBARD BUILDING. THIS IS BECAUSE THERE IS A MODEL OF TINTIN AND SNOWY ON ITS ROOF.

38

© REDING

Jari et le plan Z-Une histoire du journal Tintin, REDING

Jari and Jimmy Torrent, two young tennis champions are going through Brussels for an interview in the Tintin building. A huge crowd is waiting for them and listening to a radio presenter who is broadcasting from the roof of the building, under the gigantic head of Tintin. The following morning Jari and Jimmy go to the Belgian coast where they have to make a film to promote tennis. There they find themselves deeply involved in a counterfeiter's scam. The representation of the Éditions du Lombard building is used as a departure point and scene of the action in the story. Before being published by Éditions du Lombard, the adventure of *Jari et le plan Z (Jari and Plan Z)* were published in the *Tintin* comic.

RAYMOND REDING
[1920]

The artist and comic storywriter Raymond Reding started to make comic strips for *Récréation*, a supplement of the Belgian daily *La Dernière Heure*. After that, he worked on the *Tintin* comic. Raymond Reding, who is passionate about sport, started specialising in comic strips featuring sporting themes. His heroes have included characters like Vincent Larcher the talented footballer and Jari the top-notch tennis player.

ÉDITIONS DU LOMBARD

As a result of the work of the editor, Raymond Leblanc, Éditions du Lombard was founded in 1946 at the time of the publication of the first issues of the *Tintin* comic. The company very quickly made a place for itself in the market for the publishing of comic strips. It also became a virtually unavoidable rite of passage for Belgian (and even foreign) artist-designers and storyline writers. At the beginning, Éditions du Lombard only published stories in the *Tintin* comic. As a result of growing demand from the readers, the company started the publication of entire stories in book-form. The aims of Éditions du Lombard were, from the beginning, to 'create heroes who identified with and defended positive values', to 'disseminate captivating comic strip series that were suitable to entertain the majority' and to 'bring escapism and relaxation to all young comic strip enthusiasts aged from 7 to 77.

Currently, Éditions du Lombard has over 800 titles representing almost 50 series of collections with a wide range of genres. These are divided into prestige book series such as 'Signé', '3ᵉ vague Lombard', '3ᵉ degré Lombard', 'Polyptyque' or 'Petits Délires'. Among the comic strip heroes who have been published by Lombard, we should mention Thorgal, Ric Hochet, Léonard, Yakari, the Schtroumpfs, Alpha, Vlad, Koda, pupil Ducobu etc.

ÉDITIONS DARGAUD

Georges Dargaud founded the Éditions Dargaud in 1943. Initially it was a distribution organisation and publisher of newspapers, but Dargaud then diversified radically. In 1960 the company bought the *Pilote* magazine which had been launched a few months earlier by a group of independent writers who would later bring fame to the publishing house with their bestsellers like *Astérix*, *Blueberry* and *Tanguy et Laverdure*. From 1961 onwards, Dargaud started producing comic books at the same time.

After the first *Astérix*, with a print-run of 6,000, the early series books were published that would go round the world and make the comic strips popular. From *Achille Talon* to *Iznogoud*, from *Valérian* to *Blueberry*, from *XIII* to *Blake et Mortimer*, from *Fred* to *Boule et Bill*, from *Lucky Luke* to *Pin-Up*.....Dargaud offers a wonderful voyage in this marvellous country called 'the imagination'.

Walk under the Gare du Midi railway bridge. Keep going along the boulevard and cross the Rue de la Terre Neuve.

39

100 metres further on, on the boulevard to on your left you will see the mural called *Le Chat (The Cat)* by Philippe Geluck.

This mural attempts a visual integration with the built environment. On the one hand, the Cat reflects the shape of the wall of the house, but he also plays the role of 'Skieven Architek'. This is a Flemish expression from the Marolles area which means the 'mad architect with outrageous projects'. Here he is building himself on the wall, brick by brick.

PHILIPPE GELUCK
[1954]

Philippe Geluck is a storyline writer, artist and comedian. Having finished his studies as a comedian at the College of Advanced Media Studies in Brussels (INSAS), he began his collaboration with the French-speaking Belgian TV and Radio Network (RTBF). This work spanned twenty-one years and engendered more than 1,500 programmes such as *Lollipop, L'Esprit de famille* and the *Jeu des dictionnaires* which itself engendered *Docteur G répond à vos questions*. As for the famous *Cat*, he was created in 1982 on the thank-you note that Philippe Geluck had sent to the people who had come to his wedding. Since that time, *Le Chat* has appeared on the pages of *Le Soir* newspaper, as well as in the French and European press. So far, eleven books in total have been published by Éditions Casterman. Since 1992, Philippe Geluck has also appeared on French radio programmes. He can also be heard on Europe 1 and seen on France 2 in his 'Vivement dimanche prochain' programme that is produced by Michel Drucker as well as 'On a tout essayé' by Laurent Ruquier.

Go down the first road on your left, the Rue des Tanneurs. Then, follow the second road on the right, the Rue du Chevreuil.

40

On the right you can admire the *Boule et Bill* mural by Rob. Boule, a mischievous little boy, lives with his parents in the company of his dog and friend, Bill. The mural represents Boule and Bill coming back from the Place du Jeu de Balle along the Rue du Chevreuil. Roba has created the atmosphere rather than an accurate depiction of the setting.

ROBA
[1930]

Roba, the artist and scriptwriter, started out as a designer in advertising. After that, he worked for the *Spirou* comic where the first Boule and Bill stories were published. They were presented as short stories and jokes a single comic strip. Roba rejoined Éditions Dargaud in 1987. He involves us in the daily lives of a suburban family. Through these characters, the clumsy handyman father, perfect mother, the son Boule and his dog Bill, Roba gives us the humour that comes from everyday life.

KEEP WALKING ALONG UNTIL YOU REACH THE PLACE DU
JEU DE BALLE. ON YOUR LEFT THERE IS THE GALIA HOTEL
AND ITS BAR WITH A COMIC STRIP THEME. STOP IN THE
CENTRE OF THE SQUARE.

41

The Adventures of Tintin: The Unicorn's Secret, HERGÉ

©HERGÉ /MOULINSART 2004 / CASTERMAN

Four artists provide very different views of the Jeu de Balle square.
However the 'old market' atmosphere is present in all of them.

Hergé, however, does not provide any design details that would
allow the reader to place his hero in the Place du Jeu de Balle. He
only indicates the locality in the dialogue box at the top of one of
the illustrations in the same strip. Hergé puts the emphasis on the
atmosphere, allowing an international aspect for Tintin. In *The
Unicorn's Secret,* Tintin is walking with Snowy in the Place du Jeu de

Balle. Having met Dupont and Dupond, he discovers the model of a boat and buys it for Captain Haddock. When he gets home he puts the model down, but Snowy knocks it over and the central mast is broken. The Captain discovers that the model is the reproduction of

HERGÉ
[1907-1983]

The comic scriptwriter and artist Hergé can be considered to be one of the key figures in European comic strip design. Through his work he gives us a reflection of his era. His pseudonym comes from the initials of his first name and surname, Rémy Georges. (In French, the letters R and G are pronounced 'er gé' with 'er' pronounced 'air', and a soft 'g' as in 's' in 'measure'). Hergé's career started in 1928 when he was made the editor-in-chief of the first issue of *Le Petit Vingtième*, the weekly supplement of *Le Vingtième Siècle* paper. This publication was directed towards young people. The adventures of *Tintin aux Pays des Soviets (Tintin in Russia)* first appeared in 1929 in a copy of *Le Petit Vingtième* supplement. The first three books (*Tintin aux Pays des Soviets, Tintin au Congo, Tintin en Amérique*) were published by *Le Petit Vingtième* from 1930 onwards. In 1934, Casterman gained exclusive publishing rights for the Tintin adventures. In 1930, the first *Quick et Flupke* stories appeared in *Le Petit Vingtième*. They would only come out in book form some years later. In 1934, Hergé met a young Chinese man, Tchang Tchong-Jen, a student at the Académie des Beaux-Arts in Brussels. This young man led Hergé to understand the need to find out more about the different countries that he referred to in his work. Right up to his death, Hergé remained active in the world of comic strips and continued to inspire numerous young artists. In his books, he conveyed a lot of personal opinions and these involved him in various controversies.

The Unicorn, the boat that was sailed by his ancestor, Haddock the Knight, in the reign of Louis XIV. Then, having been away from home, Tintin finds that his flat has been turned upside down and realises that the model of the *Unicorn* has been stolen. While he is sorting things out he comes upon an old piece of parchment which reveals part of the secret of the *Unicorn*.

Une aventure de Bob Morane : Snake, CORIA - VERNES

Coria in *Snake* gives us a very realistic presentation of the Place du Jeu de Balle, both in terms of the atmosphere and the design of the fire station.

In *Bubbly Brussels*, Barelli and the Inspector talk about the stolen script (see stage 16) while walking through the Place du Jeu de Balle. By coincidence, they find an old version of the text in the square. In the background, Bob de Moor gives a close-up, but simplified, view of the Church of the Immaculate Conception. In this strip, neither the clock nor the bells are shown, and the central stained glass window is single, whereas in reality it is double.

Barelli's Adventures: Bubbly Brussels, Bob DE MOOR

PENDANT DES SEMAINES DANIEL JAUNES VIVRA SEUL, FRÉQUENTANT LES CAFÉS DE LA PLACE DU JEU DE BALLE OÙ LA GUEUZE ET LA BIÈRE BLANCHE COULENT À FLOTS.

Jaunes : Le transfert slave, BUCQUOY - TITO

© 1986 EDITIONS GLÉNAT

In *Le transfert slave (The Czech Exchange)*, Inspector Daniel Jaunes, still relieved of his duties, spends his days in the cafés in the Place du Jeu de Balle. In this illustration, the corner of the square (in the direction that you have walked from) is shown accurately, and in detail. One morning, the Inspector meets Maria, one of his former girlfriends, who has set up her medical surgery there. He collapses under the effects of alcohol and exhaustion. Maria takes him to her home. During the course of their conversation, she talks to Jaunes about her boyfriend, a young Czech who is President of the Czechoslovak Youth Union. He has been forbidden to leave his country to come back to her. At this stage, Daniel Jaunes does not yet know that during his next mission he will be in contact with Maria's friend (see the synopsis at stage 7).

WALK THE LENGTH OF THE SQUARE AND TAKE THE RUE
LA PLUME (THE ROAD IN THE MIDDLE, STRAIGHT AHE
OF YOU). AT THE T JUNCTION, TAKE THE RUE PIEREMA
TO THE LEFT

42

On your right, you will see the *Jojo* mural by Geerts.

The mural represents a vertical section of a house: 'Mamy' is in the kitchen on the ground floor, and Jojo and his friend Gros Louis are playing in the bedroom on the first floor. Geerts has included several Brussels' icons in the work: in the kitchen the calendar shows St. Michel bringing down the dragon, in the bedroom the Atomium is on the bookcase and there is a little Brussels' tram running along the floor.

ANDRÉ GEERTS
[1955]

The artist and storyline writer André Geerts started work in 1974 as an artist on the *Le Soir Jeunesse* paper. In 1983 he created *Jojo* in the *Spirou* comic. Jojo is a small boy who lives in the country with his grandmother. The first *Jojo* book was published in 1985 by Éditions Dupuis.

GO UP THE RUE PIEREMANS AND CROSS THE RUE BLAES. AT THE END OF THE RUE PIEREMANS, FOLLOW THE RUE HAUTE TO YOUR LEFT. IN THIS ROAD, AT THE CROSSROADS WITH THE RUE DES CAPUCINS (THE THIRD ON THE LEFT), ON A FAÇADE, YOU WILL SEE THE *QUICK AND FLUPKE* MURAL BY HERGÉ.

43

Quick and Flupke, the 'ketjes' (Brussels' youngsters), enliven one of the most traditionally typical areas of the city: Les Marolles. This is where the children behave in a thoughtless way which frequently has consequences for the local policeman. He, 'Agent 15', is wearing his 1930s uniform. Unlike Hergé's other characters, the children do not travel and are not involved in great adventures. Their exploits are limited to the streets of Brussels, school, an unspecified open space or a public garden. This backdrop does not in any way detract from their strong personality. Quick and Flupke are imaginative characters, ingenious tinkers who brim over with goodwill, even if they frequently become the victims of their altruism.

QUICK ET FLUPKE – HERGÉ. © MOULINSART / PHOTO: © DANIEL FOUSS, CBBD

STAY ON THE SAME ROAD FOR ANOTHER 500 METRES. TO
YOUR RIGHT YOU WILL SEE BREUGHEL L'ANCIEN SQUARE.
CROSS IT AND WHEN YOU REACH THE OTHER END, TAKE
THE RUE DES MINIMES TO YOUR RIGHT. GO UP ONE OF THE
SLOPES THAT LEAD TO THE BOTTOM OF THE PALAIS DE
JUSTICE (THE LAW COURTS). YOU CAN ALSO REACH THE

44

BRUXELLES, 20 DÉCEMBRE 1938, L'APRÈS-MIDI S'AVANCE...

© CASTERMAN

Le réseau Madou, GOFFIN - RIVIÈRE

From up here you will get an impressive view over Brussels.

In *Le Réseau Madou (The Madou Network)*, an illustration of Brussels serves
as the introduction to identify the era and location of the story. As the
action takes place in 1938, the large buildings that were constructed
from the 1960s onwards are of course not included. The hero, Thierry
Laudacieux, is a great comic strip fan. He meets a friend, Isidore Hogier
who is the head of the Madou counter-espionnage network. Madou is the
last comic strip featuring Nick and Rudy, drawn by Eddy Morgan for
the *Le Soir* newspaper. While preparing for his scout camp,
Laudacieux learns in the manual for the perfect scout to track and
follow enemies and to break coded messages. This is how he finds out
that the comic strips that are published in *Le Soir* in code. He
tells Isidore Hogier about this and he breaks the network.

ALAIN GOFFIN
[1956]

Alain Goffin, an artist and storyline writer,
received his training in comic strips at
the Saint-Luc Institute in Brussels. In
1981, he produced the *Thierry
Laudacieux* series with the writer
François Schuiten. He drew *Plagiat!* In
1989, based on a storyline by François
Schuiten and Benoît Peeters.

Gord, while looking for his friend Abla, goes to the 'pajuju', the Palais de Justice, where she is taken by 'Flipper', the arms' dealer, to be handed over to his enemy 'La Fêlée'. Gord finds this woman and sets Abla free. They then clamber up to the top of the Palais de Justice and escape in a Deltaplane, flying towards the Grand-Place. There, they find temporary refuge in the tower of the Hôtel de Ville. In spite of the rather futuristic aspect that Franz gives this comic strip, he depicts the buildings from the angle that you can now see. On the right-hand side of 'La Fêlée' you can see the Grand-Place under water, the tower of the Hôtel de Ville above the water and an almost submerged Maison du Roi. Directly below the Deltaplane, the Koekelberg Basilica is visible.

Gord, Le spit du Snack, FRANZ - DENAYER

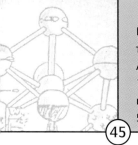

FROM HERE YOU CAN ALSO SEE THE ATOMIUM IN THE DISTANCE, TO THE LEFT OF THE HÔTEL DE VILLE. THIS IS IRON ATOM IS THE SYMBOL OF THE UNIVERSAL EXHIBITION OF 1958, AND IS FREQUENTLY DEPICTED IN COMIC STRIPS, ESPECIALLY IN THE WEEKLY PAPERS FROM THE END OF THE 50S AND 60S.

(45)

Atomium 58 is the third volume of *L'Inconnu de la Tamise (The Unknown Man from the Thames)*. In 1958, Brussels was preparing to welcome the whole world to its Universal Exhibition. In the story, while the Atomium was being completed, a group of archaeologists and journalists were searching for Inca treasure and fortifications in Peru. They were caught and locked up in a sordid dungeon in the middle of the Amazon jungle by a group of terrorists who were organising attacks in Europe. Having discovered that the next target is the Atomium, they attempt to escape by any possible means. Finally they get back to Europe in a DC3. Once in Brussels, a list of terrorists is discovered and the explosion before the arrival of the King is avoided, as a result of last-minute action.

At the beginning of *Ordre nouveau? (A New Order?)*, Inspector Daniel Jaunes's mother has just died and he asks the Rabbi to come to give her a blessing. As he leaves her house, the Rabbi is beaten up by extremists. Daniel defends him and kills one of his attackers with his service weapon. The Commissioner then asks him to hand in his resignation. While he is looking through the documents that his mother has left, Daniel discovers that his older brother, who he has never known, was an active member of the extreme right. In the illustration, a group of extremists are making plans at the base of the Atomium. Bucquoy and Tito are attempting to make the reader aware of the risks of a new rise of fascism.

BAUDOUIN DE VILLE
[1956]

The artist and storyline writer, Baudouin de Ville, took courses at the Saint-Gilles Academy in Brussels. He worked on graphics for advertising before he re-read the complete works of Hergé and E. P. Jacobs. From 1984 onwards he produced the *Inconnu de la Tamise* series and had great success with them. Four years later, he drew a new series, *Les esclaves de la torpeur* based on a storyline by Alain Streng.

Jaunes : Ordre nouveau ?, BUCQUOY - TITO

L'inconnu de la Tamise : Atomium 58, de VILLE Baudouin

IF YOU WALK SLIGHTLY BACK ON YOURSELF, YOU WILL SEE THE PALAIS DE LA JUSTICE (LAW COURTS) IN ITS ENTIRETY.

46

Une aventure de Gérard Craan : Au Dolle Mol, SANTI - BUCQUOY

This is the Brussels building that is most frequently depicted in comic strips, whether they are realistic, futuristic or humorous. This building that dominates the entire city was built between 1866 and 188, designed by the architect Poelaert. Its dimensions are fairly impressive: it reaches a height of 104 metres at the pinnacle of the dome, with an area of 26,000 square metres! In the 19th Century, this monument was considered to be the greatest building

in the world... Today there is a suggestion that it should be awarded the title of World Heritage Monument.

In the adventures of Bob Morane *(Snake)*, Gérard Craan *(Au Dolle Mol)* or Ric Hochet *(Les témoins de Satan)*, the Palais de Justice is used as a symbol of justice, the main theme of these books.

Ric Hochet : Les témoins de Satan, TIBET - A.P. DUCHÂTEAU

Une aventure de Bob Morane : Snake, CORIA - VERNES

Gord, Le spit du Snack, FRANZ - DENAYER

Denayer offers an imaginary view of the Palais de Justice and its surroundings. He depicts it as abandoned and partially destroyed, situated in the midst of exotic vegetation. He allows the building its main significance by presenting it as the temple of redemption and high moral values.

Schuiten also offers a futuristic view of the building and uses it to convey a message about the evolution of the built environment in Brussels. In the first illustration the Palais de Justice is being constructed. The view of the building accentuates its position overshadowing the city. The inhabitants of the Marolles, when faced with the gigantic

scale of the building, treat Poelaert as a 'schieven architek' (a crazy architect). In the second strip, time has passed, and now it is the Palais de Justice that in turn seems crushed by the scale of the modern buildings that are linked by aerial roads.

Les Cités obscures, Brüsel, SCHUITEN - PEETERS

Follow Rue Ernest Allard, at the corner of the Place Poelaert and the viewing point. Keep walking and in the Place due Sablon (opposite you when you reach the fourth road on the right).

47

Here you will find views of the upper and lower parts of the square, with beautiful illustrations of the Notre-Dame du Sablon Church. This was built in the 15th Century in Gothic style.

Marc Sleen in *De roos van Sakhti (Sakhti's Rose)*, conveys the atmosphere of the Sablon square in spite of the simplified representation

De avonturen van Nero : De roos van Sakhti, Marc SLEEN

Michel Vaillant : Racing-Show, Jean GRATON

that he gives of the area. In this adventure, Néro's son, Adhémar, returns from India. On the plane on the way back home, he discovers the pretty goddess Sakhti. She tells him that she is going to Belgium to visit the country to try the local specialities like french fries, beer and chocolates. In exchange for helping her, she offers Adhémar an enchanted rose. It may bring happiness, but the slightest prick from one of its thorns brings dramatic consequences. One of Néro's friends, Tuizentfloot, pricks himself. From that moment on, everything he touches turns into gold. Ricardo the Mafioso immediately sees an interest in this for him and kidnaps Tuizentfloot. The detective Van Zwam picks up his trail in the antique shops in the Sablon. After numerous escapades the rose wilts and everything returns to normality.

Jean Graton uses the Sablon square in part of his car-chase between Bob Cramer and the Brussels police. The book dates from 1985 so Graton shows the square as it was at that time, before it was re-designed. Nowadays, parking spaces and public spaces fill the centre.

WALK ACROSS THE PLACE DU SABLON AND GO TO THE RIGHT OF THE CHURCH. STOP AT THE TRAFFIC LIGHTS.

48

On the other side of the Rue de la Régence, there is the Petit Sablon. This small green area accommodates the statues that were made in 1890 by the architect Beyaert. The small statues represent the 48 trades of the Middle Ages. They are supported on Gothic columns, each one different from the next.

Gertrude au pays des Belges, STEEMAN - MALIK

In one of the funny parts of *Gertrude aux Pays des Belges*, with a storyline by Stéphane Steeman and illustrated by Malik, Gertrude guides American tourists in Brussels. The city is therefore at the centre of the story.

From the Rue de la Régence, there is an excellent view of the Palais de Justice to your right. The building is reproduced in a realistic way by Graton and Francq (see below).

49

Michel Vaillant : Racing-Show, Jean GRATON

In *Racing Show*, the Palais de Justice only plays a decorative role as a backdrop for Bob Cramer as he races in front of it at the wheel of his red Mercedes.

Des villes et des femmes (tome I), FRANCQ - DE GROOT

In *Des villes et des femmes (Towns and Women)* there is an explosion in one part of Brussels and a cloud of smoke rises behind the Palais de Justice. This explosion accentuates the anxiety of our heroine Agnès, whose husband Éric is a bomb-disposal expert in the army. Because she is frightened of a fatal accident happening, she tries to persuade him to stop his bomb-disposal work. Having lost patience, she decides to commit suicide and turns the gas on in her house. At the moment when Éric rings the doorbell, the house explodes and the two heroes are killed.

PHILIPPE FRANCQ
[1961]

The artist Philippe Francq sketched the first strips of a comic strip that was based on a storyline by Gabrielle Borile. Unfortunately, the project was never completed. He worked briefly with Bob de Moor at the Hergé Studios. In 1987, Philippe Franq completed the first episode of the *Des villes et des femmes* series in collaboration with the storyline writer Bob de Groot. He is also the artist of the famous *Largo Winch* series.

BOB DE GROOT
[1941]

Bob de Groot, the storyline writer and artist, received an art training in a specialised higher technical college. He worked on the *Félix* series and drew several hundred pages for the weekly supplements of the daily newspapers. At the beginning of the 1970s, he changed career direction and began specialising in the writing of comic strip storylines. He has worked with Dany, Francq, Greg, Geri and Tibet. In 1996 and 1998, he wrote the stories for the eighth and eleventh *Ran-Tan-Plan* series, drawn by Leonardo Vittorio.

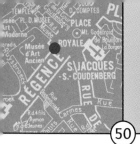

This is the starting point for the car-chase between Bob Cramer and the Brussels police.

Michel Vaillant : Racing-Show, Jean GRATON

L'inconnu de la Tamise : Atomium 58, Baudouin de VILLE

TAKE THE RUE DE LA RÉGENCE TOWARDS THE PLACE
ROYALE (ON THE LEFT). YOU WILL WALK IN FRONT OF THE
MUSÉES ROYAUX DES BEAUX-ARTS DE BELGIQUE (ROYAL
FINE ART MUSEUM), AGAIN, ON THE LEFT. WHEN YOU
REACH THE PLACE ROYAL, WALK ALONG THE LEFT-HAND
SIDE.

(51)

Marc Sleen and Baudouin de Ville offer very different interpretations
of the Place Royale.

In this illustration, the statue of Godefroi de Bouillon has been replaced
by the statue of Nero, the book's hero. We can see the Saint-Jacques-
Sur-Coudenberg Church in the background. To remind you, Schuiten
showed the bell-tower in his *Le Passage* mural. In this adventure with
Nero, the Place Royale is at the centre of the action. Because the statue
of Godefroi de Bouillon has disappeared, Nero decides to replace it with
a statue of himself in the hope of getting himself noticed. This action
does not have the desired effect, so he decides to look in the air in the
direction of the statue. The passers-by are intrigued and do the same
thing, and they lose their heads, one by one.

In *Atomium 58*, on the other hand, Baudoin de Ville includes the Place
Royale in a very realistic way. Saturnin, a journalist for *Le Crépuscule*
paper, is waiting for an informant at the foot of Godefroi de Bouillon's
statue. In exchange for financial compensation, the informant is going
to give Saturnin a list of people who are suspected of being involved
with the terrorist organisation.

De avonturen van Nero : Man van Europa, Marc SLEEN

Bucquoy and Tito offer a view of the Rue Royale looking towards the Parc Royal.

Aux limites du réel (At the Limits of Reality) takes us into a fantasy adventure where Inspector Daniel Jaunes receives his nomination as Assistant Commisioner in Dinant. The letter, dated 6th November 1938, is accompanied by a Rex business card. Rex was an extremist right-wing political party before the World War II. Daniel is even more surprised as he had not been born in 1938. However, he goes to Dinant. On the train, a woman tells him about the torture that her son experienced before being killed by the Nazis, and she warns him to be cautious about the new order. In Dinant, several events disorientate our hero: fires, delusions, extremist social gatherings etc. Daniel is finally brought back to Brussels without knowing what had really happened to him.

In the comic strips in this book, the views of Brussels serve as an introduction. They create the impression of the autumnal atmosphere of the setting.

Jaunes : Aux limites du réel, BUCQUOY - TITO

CROSS THE PLACE DES PALAIS AND WALK TOWARDS THE GATES TO THE PARC ROYAL.

53

Une grande aventure de Spirou et Fantasio : Il y a un sorcier à Champignac, André FRANQUIN

The illustration shows one of the Brussels' Park gates. It is taken from *Il y a un Sorcier à Champignac (There is a Sorcerer in Champignac)* in the adventures of Spirou and Fantasio. The park is one of the scenes of the action. The Count of Champignac has invented a magic potion which is capable of making him ten times stronger. During a walk in the Parc de Bruxelles in the company of Spirou and Fantasio, the potion is stolen by a grocer who has recognised him and heard their conversation. Spirou and Fantasio start pursuing the thief. The grocer runs off through one of the park gates (see the illustration). Franquin does not specify the location in the text, but several elements allow us to identify the spot: lamp standards, traffic lights, the columns at the gates and the statues (see stage 57).

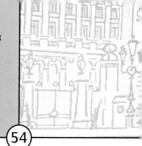

THE PALAIS ROYAL (THE ROYAL PALACE) IS TO YOUR
RIGHT, OPPOSITE THE PARC DE BRUXELLES.

54

Gertrude au pays des Belges, STEEMAN - MALIK

ANDRÉ FRANQUIN
[1924-1997]

Franquin, the scriptwriter and artist, started his career in the CBA comic strip production studio where he met Morris, Peyo and Paape in 1944. He started working for Editions Dupuis in 1946, but after a difference of opinion with the publisher, worked simultaneously for the *Spirou* and *Tintin* comics. He created the Gaston Lagaffe, Marsupiami, Modeste and Pompon characters. From 1948 to 1969, he devoted himself entirely to Spirou and Fantasio before focussing his work on the Gaston Lagaffe adventures. Franquin's designs are 'lively and expressive'. He was undoubtedly one of the key influences of Editions Dupuis and European comic strip art.

The current appearance of the Royal Palace is the result of a restoration which was undertaken by King Léopold II by Henri Maquet from 1904-9. He gave the façade of the building its Louis XVI style, which is both formal and imposing.

Above, Gertrude is once again introducing Brussels to American tourists.

125

GO INTO THE PARC ROYAL AND STOP AT THE OTHER SIDE OF THE GATES, LOOKING TOWARDS THE ROYAL PALACE.

55

Les maîtres de l'orge : Noël 1932, VAN HAMME - VALLES

Francis Vallès, in *Les Maîtres de l'orge: Noël 1932 (The Barley Masters: Noël 1932)* drew the view between the Parc de Bruxelles with the Palais de Justice, passing Godefroi de Bouillon, in the middle of the Place Royale. This line goes on through the Parc de Bruxelles along the diagonal pathway through the park behind you. This representation is extremely realistic, even if the perspective seems to be somewhat diminished. Brussels occupies a rather unimportant place in this comic strip. This view serves as a backdrop to a business meeting which takes place in a building that is located to the right of the gates to the Parc Royal.

The *Maîtres de l'orge* series features a dynasty of Belgian beer-makers,

the Steenforts. In the middle of the 19th Century, Charles Steenfort, a young novice in an Abbey that has a brewery, meets Adrienne, his future wife. He realises that his greatest wish is to make beer and he returns to his native village in order to open a brewery with his childhood friend, Frans Texel. He does his utmost to make a success in the beer-making industry. His victory in the competition for the best beer at the annual beer festival in Brabant, is the starting point for the building of the Steenfort empire which lasted from 1954 to 1997.

JEAN VAN HAMME
[1939]

FRANCIS VALLÈS
[1959]

The artist and storyline writer Francis Vallès, started his career in comic strips in 1983 when Éditions Magic-Strip published his book *Le lac des fous*. He adapted several literary works for comic strips, such as *Les voyages de Gulliver* and *20 000 lieues sous les mers*. In 1992, Francis Vallès worked collaboratively with the storyline writer Jean Van Hamme on the *Maîtres de l'orge* saga (published by Éditions Glénat).

Jean Van Hamme, the novelist and storyline writer, became well-known in 1968 with the storylines for *Modeste et Pompon*. He wrote the *Époxy* stories for Paul Cuvelier, as well as the sixth and seventh episodes of *Corentin*. He created *Thorgal* with the artist Grzegorz Rosinski in 1977. In 1992, he wrote *Les maîtres de l'orge* with Francis Vallès. He adapted this series for serialisation on television for the RTBF (Belgian TV and Radio) and France 2. In addition, Jean Van Hamme wrote a version of the story as a novel that was published by Robert Laffont. He is also the writer of the *XIII* and *Largo Winch* series of comic books.

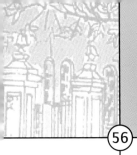

The Brussels Park, situated between the Royal Palace and the Parliament building, was officially made 'public' in 1775. The Park as we know it today is the work of Joachim Zinner and Barnabé Guimard. It is worth remembering that it played an important role as the battle-ground for the Belgian revolutionary forces as well as for the Dutch armies of William of Orange during the 'glorious days' that led up to Belgian independence in 1830.

The illustration below, an introduction to one of the Inspector Daniel Jaunes adventures, offers a very realistic view of the Park.

Jaunes : Aux limites du réel, BUCQUOY - TITO

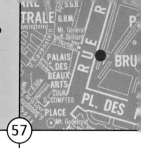

Une grande aventure de Spirou et Fantasio : Il y a un sorcier à Champignac, André FRANQUIN

In *Il y a un sorcier à Champignac (There is a Sorcerer in Champignac)*, Spirou et Fantasio attempt to catch the grocer before he gets out of the Park (see stage 53). They run round the statues as fast as they can. These are on the right-hand side of the pathway at right-angles to the path that you have just left.

CROSS THE RUE ROYALE AND WALK DOWN THE STEPS ON THE RUE BARON HORTA, OPPOSITE YOU. AT THE CROSS-ROADS, CROSS THE RUE RAVENSTEIN AND STOP. BEHIND YOU, AT THE JUNCTION OF THE RUES RAVENSTEIN AND BARON HORTA, YOU WILL SEE THE PALAIS DES BEAUX-ARTS (THE ART GALLERY AND CONCERT HALL).

58

Barelli's Adventures: Bubbly Brussels, Bob DE MOOR

In *Bubbly Brussels*, the Palais des Beaux-Arts acts as a backdrop to the Barelli's aunt's conversation.

The Palais des Beaux-Arts, opened in 1928, is the work of the architect Victor Horta. He placed a spacious concert hall in the centre of this building that is devoted to culture. The concert hall fills the building's entire height (three floors) and is the centrepiece of the entire building around it. The acoustics are perfect, and the hall can accommodate 2,200 people. This is why the well-known Concours Reine Élizabeth (Queen Elizabeth Competition) is held here.

The construction of the Palais des Beaux-Arts brought great technical difficulties: firstly, the difference in levels between the Rue Royale and the Rue Ravenstein is considerable. Also, on the Rue Royale side, it would have been unthinkable to build a grandiose façade that would have been a contradiction to the neo-classical aspect of the square or the Royal Palace. Such a construction would also have impeded the panoramic view of the city from the Place des Palais.

Follow the Rue Ravenstein (to the left of the arcades of the same name). After that, go down the right-hand side of the Mont des Arts steps, or walk down the Rue des Sols.

59

Gertrude au pays des Belges, STEEMAN - MALIK

The extract from *Gertrude au pays des Belges* below provides an illustration of the Mont des Arts in its original form.

In the comic strip *Souvenirs (Memories)*, Stéphane Steeman takes the opportunity to show the refurbishment of the Mont des Arts. The conversation bubble is self-explanatory. The gardens that are represented here

date from 1909. They were later replaced by a 'French' garden containing a predominance of rock. The gardens are surrounded by the Bibliothèque royale and the Palais des Congrès. The equestrian statue of King Abert I dominates the lower esplanade. A recent renovation phase of the gardens has been completed to redevelop the Mont des Arts in a very different style, restoring its status as a garden in the centre of the city.

BELOW YOU, ON TOP OF THE ARCADE, THERE IS AN ORIGINAL
CLOCK THAT IS BROUGHT TO LIFE BY ITS GROUP OF
TRADITIONAL AND HISTORICAL FIGURES. YOU ARE NOW
REACHING THE PLACE DE L'ALBERTINE. CROSS THE
CANTERSTEEN AND THE BOULEVARD DE L'IMPÉRATRICE.
WALK ALONG THE BOULEVARD TO YOUR RIGHT AND KEEP

60

On your right, on the other side of the boulevard, you will see the Gare
Centrale (Central Station) which was designed by Victor Horta as part
of the plan to build the Nord-Midi (North-South) railway junction.

In this adventure with Nero, (see below), we find the two heroes
Petoetje and Petatje going to the Central Station to take a train for
Antwerp. They want to buy white cockerels there as an offering for
Singbonga, an Indian fakir who Nero had found at his home one day.
This fakir is considered to be a sun god who will remain with those
who give him offerings.

De avonturen van Nero : Singbonga, Marc SLEEN

WALKING UNTIL YOU REACH THE CARREFOUR DE L'EUROPE (100 METRES). STOP AT THE TRAFFIC LIGHTS.

BY STAYING ON THE BOULEVARD DE L'IMPÉRATRICE, YOU WILL REACH THE SAINTS-MICHEL-ET-GUDULE CATHEDRAL.

[The telephone numbers include the 0032 international dialling code for Belgium. 02 is the dialling code for Brussels if you are already in Belgium. If you are phoning from outside Belgium, the numbers have 12 digits, excluding the 0 before the Brussels dialling code 2 eg. 0032 2 219 19 80 for the Comic Strip Centre].

MUSEUMS

Le Centre belge de la Bande dessinée (Belgian Comic Strip Centre)
Specialised library, museum, restaurant
Rue des Sables 20, 1000 Brussels
Tel: 0032 (0)2 219 19 80
www.comicscenter.net

Le Musée Jijé
Rue du Houblon 43, 1000 Brussels
Tel: 0032 (0)2 513 33 04
www.jijé.org

WEBSITES

City of Brussels Website
www.bruxelles.be

Brussels-Capital Region Website
www.bruxelles.irisnet.be

for a Website offering several links: everything that is going on in the Comic Strip world
www.brusselsBDtour.com

BOOKSHOP-GALLERIES IN BRUSSELS

Slumberland
Rue des Sables 20, 1000 Brussels
Tel: 0032 (0)2 219 58 01

Brüsel
Boulevard Anspach 100, 1000, Brussels
Tel: 0032 (0)2 511 08 09
www.brusel.com

La Bulle d'or
Boulevard Anspach 124, 1000 Brussels
Tel: 0032 (0)2 513 72 35
www.multibd.com

Multi BD
Boulevard Anspach 126-128, 1000 Brussels
Tel: 0032 (0)2 513 01 86
www.multibd.com

Tropismes Jeunesse et BD
Galerie du Roi 11, 1000 Brussels
Tel: 0032 (0)2 511 56 51
www.tropismes.com

Het B-Gevaar
Rue de la Fourche 126-128, 1000 Brussels
Tel: 0032 (0)2 513 14 86
www.b-gevaar.com

Petits Papiers
Boulevard Lemonnier 15, 1000 Brussels
Tel: 0032 (0)2 514 68 04

Little Nemo
Boulevard Lemonnier 25, 1000 Brussels
Tel: 0032 (0)2 514 68 04

Le Fantôme Espagnol
Boulevard Lemonnier 71, 1000 Brussels
Tel: 0032 (0)2 512 32 04

L'Idée Fixe
Boulevard Lemonnier 131, 1000 Brussels
Tel: 0032 (0)2 513 92 22

Malpertuis
Rue des Éperonniers 18, 1000 Brussels
Tel: 0032 (0)2 512 83 00

Le Dépôt
Rue du Midi 108, 1000 Brussels
Tel: 0032 (0)2 513 04 84
www.depotbd.com

Utopia-Gallery
Rue des Renards 16, 1000 Brussels
Tel: 0032 (0)475 81 75 10
www.utopia-gallery.com

Only You / BD Stars
Place du Jeu de Balle 79, 1000 Brussels
Tel: 0032 (0)475 69 75 38

MURALS that are not included on the walk

Nero, Marc SLEEN, Place Saint-Géry

Cori le moussaillon, Bob DE MOOR, rue des Fabriques

Les rêves de Nic, HERMANN, rue des Fabriques

Lucky Luke, MORRIS, rue de la Buanderie

Isabelle, WILL, rue de la verdure

Olivier Rameau, DANY, rue du Chêne

Blondin et Cirage, JIJÉ, rue des Capucins

Le Jeune Albert, CHALAN, rue des Alexiens

Monsieur Jean, DUPUY & BERBERIAN, rue des Bogarts

L'archange, YSLAIRE, rue des Chartreux

Passe moi l'ciel, STUF & Jean RY, rue des Minimes

La Patrouille des Castors, MITACQ, rue Blaes

La Marque Jaune, Edgar P. JACOBS, rue du Houblon

BARUTI Barly
Les aventures de Sako et Yannick : Objectif Terre
1994 - AGCD (Administration générale de la Coopération au Développement)

BERTHET Philippe
Couleur Café
1986 - Éditions Dupuis

BUCQUOY - TITO
Jaunes : Aux limites du réel
1986 - Éditions Glénat
Jaunes : Ordre nouveau ?
1986 - Éditions Glénat
Jaunes : Le transfert slave
1986 - Éditions Glénat

CARIN - RIVIÈRE - BORILE
Le Code Zimmerman, l'Opéra de la mort
1986 - Éditions du Lombard

CORIA - VERNES
Une aventure de Bob Morane : Snake
1989 - Éditions du Lombard

DE MOOR Bob
Barelli's Adventures: Bubbly Brussels
1990 - (produced with permission of the Ministry of Public Health and the Brussels Flemish-speaking Business Community)

de VILLE Baudouin
L'inconnu de la Tamise : Atomium 58
1986 - Éditions Récréabull

DUCHÂTEAU - HULET
Pharaon : Des ombres sur le sable
1997 - Éditions Glénat

FRANCQ - DE GROOT
Des villes et des femmes (tome I)
1987 - Éditions Dargaud

FRANQUIN André
Une grande aventure de Spirou et Fantasio : Il y a un sorcier à Champignac
1977 - Éditions Dupuis

FRANZ - DENAYER
Gord, le spit du snack
1988 - Éditions du Lombard

GOFFIN - RIVIÈRE
Le réseau Madou
1982 - Éditions Casterman

GRATON Jean
Michel Vaillant : Racing-Show
1985 - Graton éditeur

HERGÉ
Les aventures de Tintin : Le secret de la Licorne
1974 - Éditions Casterman

HULET Daniel
L'État morbide - Acte Premier : La Maison-Dieu
1987 - Éditions Glénat

JACOBS Edgar P.
The adventures of Blake and Mortimer : The Mystery of the Great Pyramid (tome I)
1986 - Éditions Dargaud

JOOS - ANDRIEU
Ostende-Miami
1984 - Éditions Ice Crim's

JUILLARD A. - SENTE Y.
Les aventures de Blake et Mortimer : Les sarcophages du 6ᵉ continent (tome I)
2003 - Éditions Blake et Mortimer / Studio Jacobs

MAGDA - LAPIÈRE
Le tueur, Charly
1997 - Éditions Dupuis

REDING
Jari et le plan Z - Une histoire du journal Tintin
1964 - Éditions du Lombard

SANTI - BUCQUOY
Une aventure de Gérard Craan : Au Dolle Mol
1982 - Éditions Michel De Ligne

SCHUITEN - PEETERS
Les Cités Obscures : Brüsel
1992 - Éditions Casterman

SLEEN Marc
De avonturen van Nero : De zwarte toren
1987 - Éditions du Standaard
De avonturen van Nero : De verloren zee
1988 - Éditions du Standaard
De avonturen van Nero : Man van Europa
1990 - Éditions du Standaard
De avonturen van Nero : Singboga
1995 - Éditions du Standaard
De avonturen van Nero : Het spook uit de zandstraat
1996 - Éditions du Standaard
De avonturen van Nero : De roos van Sakhti
1997 - Éditions du Standaard

STANISLAS - BOCQUET- FROMENTAL
Les aventures d'Hergé
1999 - Éditions Reporter

STEEMAN - MALIK
Gertrude au pays des Belges
1996 - Éditions « Nous »

TIBET - A.P. DUCHATEAU
Ric Hochet : Les témoins de satan
1989 - Éditions du Lombard
Ric Hochet : B.D. Meurtres
2000 - Éditions du Lombard

VAN HAMME - VALLÈS
Les maîtres de l'orge, Noël 1932
1995 - Éditions Glénat

VANDERSTEEN Willy
Bob et Bobette : Le Fantôme espagnol
1993 - Éditions du Standaard
Bob et Bobette : Manneken-Pis l'irascible
1988 - Éditions du Standaard

ACKNOWLEDGEMENTS

The editor and writer would like to thank the publishers as well as the artists and comic scriptwriters who have given permission for the publication of this guidebook.

The author would also like to thank Céline Corna Pellegrini, and Dr. and Sandrine Vandorselaer for their help and support that they have given in the preparation of this book. He is also grateful to the Société Immobilière des Nations for their technical support at the preparation stage of this guidebook.

With support from

Brussels City Tourist Board

Belgian Comic Strip Centre

Brussels Capital Region

Thibaut VANDORSELAER

BRUXELLES DANS LA BD

LA BD DANS BRUXELLES

----- ITINÉRAIRE DÉCOUVERTE -----

Préface de Jean VAN HAMME

Versant Sud

www.versant-sud.com